THE BLOCKCHAIN HANDBOOK: ENABLING TECHNOLOGIES AND APPLICATIONS

DR. RAJESH MAMILLA

Made with ♥ on the Notion Press Platform
www.notionpress.com

To all the pioneers, visionaries, and innovators who have relentlessly pursued the advancement of blockchain technology.

To the students, researchers, and professionals who strive to deepen their understanding and harness the transformative power of blockchain for a better, more transparent world.

And to my Wife, family and scholars, whose unwavering support and encouragement have made this work possible.

This book is dedicated to you

Contents

FOREWORD

In the rapidly evolving landscape of technology, blockchain has emerged as one of the most revolutionary advancements of our time. Its potential to transform industries, enhance security, and foster transparency is unparalleled, making it an essential area of study and application.

"The Blockchain Handbook: Enabling Technologies and Applications" serves as a comprehensive guide to understanding the multifaceted world of blockchain. This book meticulously covers the foundational concepts of blockchain technology, provides an in-depth overview of cryptography and encryption, explores the enabling technologies that power blockchain, and delves into the intricacies of distributed ledger technologies.

From the foundational aspects to the advanced topics of mining, forking, and digital signatures, this handbook is designed to be both an introductory text for beginners and a detailed reference for seasoned professionals. Each chapter is crafted to offer clear explanations, practical insights, and real-world applications, making complex concepts accessible and engaging.

As the world increasingly embraces decentralized solutions, the importance of blockchain cannot be overstated. This book aims to equip readers with the knowledge and tools necessary to navigate and contribute to this dynamic field. Whether you are a student, a researcher, a developer, or an industry professional, "The Blockchain Handbook" will guide you through the fundamental principles and cutting-edge developments that define blockchain technology today.May this book serve as a beacon of knowledge and a catalyst for innovation in the exciting journey of blockchain discovery.

Sincerely
Dr. Rajesh Mamilla

PREFACE

The advent of blockchain technology has brought forth a paradigm shift in how we think about data, security, and trust. From its inception as the underlying technology for Bitcoin, blockchain has evolved into a versatile and transformative technology with applications spanning numerous industries, including finance, supply chain, healthcare, and beyond.

This textbook, "The Blockchain Handbook: Enabling Technologies and Applications," is the culmination of extensive research, practical insights, and a deep passion for the subject. It is designed to serve as a comprehensive guide for anyone looking to understand and harness the power of blockchain technology.

Objectives of the Book

The primary goal of this book is to provide a thorough understanding of blockchain technology and its enab ling components. It covers a wide range of topics, includingOverview of Cryptography and Encryption,Blockchain as an Enabling Technology, Distributed Ledger Technologies in Blockchain,Mining, Forking, and Sales in Blockchain Technology and Digital Signatures.

This book is intended for a diverse audience:

Students and Academics: Providing foundational knowledge and advanced insights suitable for both introductory courses and in-depth studies.

Developers and Technologists: Offering practical guidance and technical details to aid in the development and implementation of blockchain solutions.

Business Professionals and Entrepreneurs: Presenting strategic perspectives on leveraging blockchain technology for innovation and competitive advantage.

Researchers and Enthusiasts: Stimulating further exploration and understanding of the potential and challenges of blockchain.

Sincerely

Dr. Rajesh Mamilla

Acknowledgements

The journey of writing this book has been both challenging and rewarding. I extend my deepest gratitude to my beloved wife,family and scholars for their unwavering support and encouragement throughout this process.

I also want to acknowledge the pioneers and innovators in the blockchain community whose groundbreaking work and relentless pursuit of excellence continue to drive this field forward. Your contributions have paved the way for the advancements I explore in this book.

Sincerely

Dr. Rajesh Mamilla

Overview of Cryptography and Encryption

LEARNING OBJECTIVES

- List the different types of cryptographic techniques
- Assess the effectiveness of cryptography in protecting data privacy
- Name the main types of encryption algorithms
- Compare different encryption standards and their applications
- Evaluate the effectiveness of different encryption algorithms in resisting known-plaintext attack

1.1 Introduction to Cryptography

Cryptography, derived from the Greek words "kryptos" meaning hidden and "graphia" meaning writing, is the science and art of securing communication and data by converting it into a format that is unintelligible to anyone except those authorized to access it. Dating back to ancient civilizations, cryptography has played a pivotal role in safeguarding sensitive information, ranging from military secrets to financial transactions, and has evolved significantly over time to meet the challenges of modern communication and information technology.

1.1.1 Definitions of Cryptography

Cryptography is the art and science of keeping messages secure.

Bruce Schneier

Cryptography is the discipline that embodies principles, means, and methods for the transformation of data in order to hide its meaning, prevent its unauthorized use, or prevent its unauthorized modification.

William Stallings

Cryptography is the practice and study of techniques for secure communication in the presence of third parties called adversaries.

Whitfield Diffie and Martin Hellman

1.1.2 Importance of Cryptography

Cryptography, the art and science of securing communication, has played a pivotal role in safeguarding sensitive information throughout history. In an increasingly digital world, where data is constantly exchanged and stored, cryptography serves as the cornerstone of modern security measures. By employing complex mathematical algorithms and techniques, cryptography ensures confidentiality, integrity, and authenticity in electronic communications and transactions.

Data Confidentiality: Cryptography enables the encryption of data, ensuring that only authorized parties can access its contents. This is crucial for protecting sensitive information such as personal data, financial transactions, and corporate secrets from unauthorized access and eavesdropping.

Data Integrity: Cryptographic techniques such as hashing allow for the verification of data integrity. By generating unique digital fingerprints (hashes) of data, cryptography helps detect any unauthorized alterations or tampering. This ensures that data remains unaltered during transmission or storage, maintaining its reliability and trustworthiness.

Authentication: Cryptography provides mechanisms for verifying the identities of parties involved in communication or transactions. Through digital signatures and certificate-based authentication, cryptography enables parties to authenticate each other's identities, mitigating the risk of impersonation and fraud.

Non-repudiation: Cryptographic signatures offer undeniable evidence regarding the source and integrity of messages or transactions. This serves to thwart any attempts by parties to disavow their participation in specific communications or dealings, thereby bolstering accountability and expediting the resolution of disputes.

Secure Communication Channels: Cryptography enables the creation of safe communication channels, even while using unsecured networks like the internet. By employing protocols such as SSL/TLS, cryptographic methods are used to encrypt data while it is being transmitted, so safeguarding it against interception and illicit access. This guarantees the confidentiality and privacy of communication among individuals.

Cryptography is essential for ensuring the security and trustworthiness of digital communications and transactions. By providing mechanisms for confidentiality, integrity, authentication, non-repudiation, and secure communication channels, cryptography forms the foundation of modern cybersecurity practices, safeguarding sensitive information and enabling secure interactions in the digital realm.

1.1.3 Historical Development

The historical development of cryptography is a fascinating journey that spans millennia, evolving from rudimentary techniques to sophisticated cryptographic systems used in modern times. Here are some major milestones in the history of cryptography:

1. Ancient Civilizations:

Egyptian Hieroglyphs: Early examples of cryptography can be found in ancient Egypt, where hieroglyphs were used to conceal messages in tombs and monuments.

Caesar Cipher: In ancient Rome, Julius Caesar is said to have used a simple substitution cipher, known as the Caesar Cipher, to encode military communications by shifting each letter in the alphabet by a fixed number of positions.

2. Medieval Europe:

Polyalphabetic Ciphers: During the Renaissance, polymath Leon Battista Alberti introduced the concept of polyalphabetic ciphers, such as the Alberti Cipher Disk, which used multiple alphabets to encode messages more securely.

Vigenère Cipher: Developed by Giovan Battista Bellaso and later popularized by Blaise de Vigenère in the 16th century, this polyalphabetic substitution cipher became widely used for secure communication among diplomats and military commanders.

3. World Wars:

Enigma Machine: In the early 20th century, the German military utilized the Enigma machine, an electromechanical rotor cipher machine, to encrypt sensitive communications during World War I and World War II. Breaking the Enigma cipher became a pivotal effort in Allied codebreaking efforts, led by mathematicians and cryptanalysts such as Alan Turing.

Navajo Code Talkers: During World War II, the Navajo Code Talkers used their native language as a code to transmit sensitive information, providing a highly secure means of communication that confounded enemy cryptanalysts.

4. Modern Cryptography:

Public-Key Cryptography: In the 1970s, Whitfield Diffie and Martin Hellman introduced the concept of public-key cryptography, revolutionizing the field by enabling secure communication over insecure channels without the need for a shared secret key.

RSA Algorithm: Developed by Ron Rivest, Adi Shamir, and Leonard Adleman in 1977, the RSA algorithm became one of the first practical implementations of public-key cryptography, laying the foundation for secure digital communication and e-commerce.

Elliptic Curve Cryptography (ECC): Introduced in the 1980s, ECC offers strong security with shorter key lengths compared to traditional cryptographic algorithms, making it well-suited for resource-constrained environments such as mobile devices and IoT devices.

5. Contemporary Developments:

"Quantum Cryptography": Quantum computing has prompted academics to investigate novel cryptography methods grounded in the laws of quantum physics. These techniques, such as quantum key distribution (QKD), have the potential to provide encryption that is theoretically impossible to crack.

Homomorphic Encryption: This nascent cryptographic technology allows for computations to be executed on data that is encrypted without the need for decryption, hence maintaining the confidentiality of the information and confidentiality in cloud computing and data analytics applications.

These historical developments in cryptography underscore its critical role in securing communications, protecting sensitive information, and advancing technological innovation throughout human history.

1.1.4 Types of Cryptography

Types of cryptographic techniques encompass various methods used to secure communication, data, and transactions. They can be broadly categorized into two main categories: symmetric key cryptography and asymmetric key cryptography.

A.**Symmetric Key Cryptography:**

Symmetric key cryptography, also known as secret key cryptography, involves the use of a single shared key for both encryption and deciphering of data. The key must remain confidential and known only to the parties involved in communication. The plaintext message is encrypted using the shared key, resulting in ciphertext. The ciphertext is decrypted back to plaintext using the same shared key.

Advantages:

- Symmetric important cryptography generally offers swifter processing speeds and demands fewer computational resources in contrast to asymmetric key cryptography.
- Implementation and management of symmetric key algorithms are relatively straightforward.

Examples of Symmetric Key Algorithms:

AES (Advanced Encryption Standard): Widely used for securing sensitive data, AES operates on fixed-size blocks of data and supports key lengths of 128, 192, or 256 bits.

DES (Data Encryption Standard): Though less commonly used due to its vulnerability to brute force attacks, DES played a crucial role in establishing the foundation for contemporary symmetric encryption protocols.

B.**Asymmetric Key Cryptography:**

Asymmetric key cryptography, also known as public-key cryptography, involves the use of a pair of keys: a public key and a private key. The keys are mathematically related, but computationally infeasible to derive one from the other. Here's how it works: The sender encrypts the plaintext message using the recipient's public key. The recipient decrypts the ciphertext using their corresponding private key.

Advantages:

- Public keys is distribution of this content can occur without constraints, thus obviating the necessity for a secure medium for key exchange..
- Asymmetric key cryptography enables the creation and verification of digital signatures, ensuring message integrity and authentication.

Examples of Asymmetric Key Algorithms:

RSA (Rivest-Shamir-Adleman): Named after its inventors, RSA is one of the most widely used asymmetric encryption algorithms, particularly for securing internet communications and digital signatures.

Elliptic Curve Cryptography (ECC): ECC offers similar security to RSA but with shorter key lengths, making it more suitable for resource-constrained environments such as mobile devices and IoT devices.

Symmetric key cryptography and asymmetric key cryptography serve complementary roles in securing data and communications. Although symmetric encryption is efficient and simple, asymmetric encryption offers key distribution and digital signature capabilities. Knowing the strengths and limitations of each type of cryptography is essential for designing secure systems and protocols in various domains, from cybersecurity to finance and beyond.

1.1.5 Cryptography Algorithms

commonly used cryptographic algorithms, categorized by their types, along with a brief description of each as shown below

Symmetric Key Algorithms

1.AES (Advanced Encryption Standard)

- **Description**: A widely used symmetric encryption algorithm that encrypts data in fixed blocks of 128 bits using keys of 128, 192, or 256 bits.
- **Use Case**: Used in various applications for secure data encryption, including file encryption and secure communications.

2. DES (Data Encryption Standard)

- **Description**: An older symmetric encryption algorithm that encrypts data in 64-bit blocks using a 56-bit key.
- **Use Case**: Historically used in many applications, now considered insecure due to its short key length.

3.Triple DES (3DES)

- **Description**: An enhancement of DES that applies the DES algorithm three times to each data block using either two or three keys.
- **Use Case**: Used in legacy systems that require higher security than DES.

4.Blowfish

- **Description**: A symmetric block cipher that encrypts data in 64-bit blocks using variable-length keys from 32 to 448 bits.
- **Use Case**: Suitable for applications where key changes are frequent, such as password hashing.

Asymmetric Key Algorithms
1.RSA (Rivest-Shamir-Adleman)

- **Description**: An asymmetric encryption algorithm that uses a pair of keys (public and private) for secure data transmission.
- **Use Case**: Widely used for secure data transmission, digital signatures, and key exchange.

2.ECC (Elliptic Curve Cryptography)

- **Description**: Uses elliptic curves over finite fields for encryption, providing equivalent security to RSA but with shorter keys.
- **Use Case**: Used in mobile devices, SSL/TLS certificates, and secure communications due to its efficiency and lower power consumption.

3.DSA (Digital Signature Algorithm)

- **Description**: An asymmetric algorithm used specifically for digital signatures.
- **Use Case**: Used to authenticate the origin and integrity of messages and documents.

Hash Functions
1.SHA-256 (Secure Hash Algorithm 256-bit)

- **Description**: A cryptographic hash function that produces a 256-bit hash value from input data.
- **Use Case**: Used in blockchain technology, digital signatures, and data integrity verification.

2.MD5 (Message Digest Algorithm 5)

- **Description**: An older hash function that produces a 128-bit hash value from input data.
- **Use Case**: Historically used for checksums and data integrity, now considered insecure due to vulnerability to hash collisions.

3.SHA-3

- **Description**: The latest member of the Secure Hash Algorithm family, providing enhanced security and different internal structure compared to SHA-2.
- **Use Case**: Used in cryptographic applications where a higher level of security is required.

Key Exchange Algorithms
1.Diffie-Hellman

- **Description**: A method for securely exchanging cryptographic keys over a public channel.
- **Use Case**: Used in protocols like SSL/TLS to securely negotiate encryption keys.

2.ECDH (Elliptic Curve Diffie-Hellman)

- **Description**: A variant of Diffie-Hellman using elliptic curve cryptography for enhanced security and efficiency.
- **Use Case**: Used in secure communications and mobile device encryption.

Digital Signature Algorithms
1.RSA (Rivest-Shamir-Adleman)

- **Description**: Besides encryption, RSA is also used for creating and verifying digital signatures.
- **Use Case**: Used for verifying the authenticity and integrity of digital messages and documents.

2.ECDSA (Elliptic Curve Digital Signature Algorithm)

- **Description**: A variant of DSA that uses elliptic curve cryptography to provide shorter keys and faster computation.
- **Use Case**: Used in secure communications, blockchain technology, and other applications requiring digital signatures.

1.1.6 Attacks on Cryptography

Attacks on Cryptography

1. **Ciphertext-Only Attack (COA)**
    - **Description**: The attacker has access only to the ciphertext and attempts to deduce the plaintext or the key.
    - **Example**: Frequency analysis in simple substitution ciphers.

2. **Known-Plaintext Attack (KPA)**

- **Description**: The attacker has access to both the plaintext and its corresponding ciphertext and attempts to deduce the key.
- **Example**: Cryptanalysis of the Enigma machine during World War-II

3. **Chosen-Plaintext Attack (CPA)**

- **Description**: The attacker can choose arbitrary plaintexts to be encrypted and obtain the corresponding ciphertexts to deduce the key.
- **Example**: Adaptive chosen-plaintext attacks on block ciphers like DES.

4. **Chosen-Ciphertext Attack (CCA)**

- **Description**: The attacker can choose arbitrary ciphertexts to be decrypted and obtain the corresponding plaintexts to deduce the key.
- **Example**: Padding oracle attacks on cryptographic protocols like SSL/TLS.

5.**Side-Channel Attack**

- **Description**: The attacker exploits physical characteristics of the cryptographic system, such as timing information, power consumption, or electromagnetic leaks, to extract the key.
- **Example**: Timing attacks on RSA implementations.

6.**Man-in-the-Middle Attack (MITM)**

- **Description**: The attacker intercepts communication between two parties and can read, alter, or inject messages without the parties knowing.
- **Example**: Attack on Diffie-Hellman key exchange.

7.**Replay Attack**

- **Description**: The attacker intercepts a valid data transmission and retransmits it to trick the receiver into unauthorized operations.
- **Example**: Replaying authentication messages to gain access to a system.

8.**Brute-Force Attack**

- **Description**: The attacker systematically tries all possible keys until the correct one is found.
- **Example**: Cracking weak passwords or short encryption keys.

9.**Cryptanalysis**

- **Description**: The study of analyzing information systems to breach cryptographic security without knowing the key.
- **Example**: Differential cryptanalysis of DES.

1.2 Encryption

Data secrecy must be protected in the linked digital world of today, when sensitive data is shared among several networks and devices. Encryption emerges as a pivotal solution in this endeavor, converting plain text into cipher text, thus making it indecipherable without the requisite decryption key. Throughout history, employing sophisticated algorithms to scramble data has been a common practice to shield sensitive communications and information from unauthorized access. Encryption plays a crucial role in protecting confidential data, including financial transactions, individual communications, and sensitive documents, from interception and unauthorized intrusion. Both people and corporations may successfully reduce the dangers of data loss, theft of identities, as well as espionage by encrypting their data, protecting their confidentiality and the integrity associated with their digital assets.

1.2.1 Definition of Encryption

Encryption is the method of encrypting information in a manner that restricts access to only authorised individuals. It serves as a fundamental tool in ensuring data confidentiality and privacy, particularly in the context of secure communication over untrusted channels.

Whitfield Diffie and Martin Hellman

Encryption is the transformation of data into a form that is incomprehensible to anyone without the proper authentication key, thereby ensuring the confidentiality and integrity of sensitive information. It is a cornerstone of secure communication and data protection in the digital age.

Tim Berners-Lee

Encryption is a crucial process that transforms data into a coded format, ensuring that access is restricted solely to authorized individuals. By transforming information into an unintelligible format, encryption becomes an essential mechanism for safeguarding data confidentiality and privacy. This is especially crucial when transmitting sensitive data over untrusted channels, where interception or unauthorized access poses a significant risk. With encryption, data is converted into a form that is incomprehensible to anyone lacking the appropriate authentication key. This not only guarantees the secrecy of the information but also preserves its integrity, thereby preventing any unauthorised alteration or tampering. Encryption is a crucial component of secure communication and data security in the digital age. It is essential for maintaining privacy standards and facilitating the secure flow of sensitive information.

1.2.2 Historical Development

Encryption is the procedure of transforming information in a manner that restricts access to only authorised individuals and has a long and rich history dating back thousands of years. Here's an overview of its historical development:

Ancient Civilizations: Encryption techniques can be traced back to ancient civilizations such as Egypt, where hieroglyphs were used to conceal messages. These early forms of encryption relied on simple substitution methods to obfuscate the meaning of the text.

Classical Ciphers: The development of classical ciphers marked a significant advancement in encryption techniques. One of the most famous examples is the Caesar Cipher, attributed to Julius Caesar, which involved shifting each letter of the alphabet by a fixed number of positions. Other classical ciphers, such as the Atbash Cipher and the Vigenère Cipher, introduced more sophisticated methods of encryption based on various substitution and transposition techniques.

Renaissance and Enlightenment Era: During the Renaissance and Enlightenment periods, cryptography became increasingly important for military and diplomatic communications. Prominent figures like Leon Battista Alberti and Blaise de Vigenère made significant contributions to the field, refining existing techniques and developing new cryptographic systems.

19th and 20th Centuries: The invention of the telegraph and later the telephone necessitated the development of more secure encryption methods to protect sensitive communications. This led to the creation of complex cipher machines such as the Enigma machine used by the German military during World War II. Cryptanalysis, the science of breaking codes and ciphers, also saw significant advancements during this period, with figures like Alan Turing playing a pivotal role in cracking Enigma and other cryptographic systems used by Axis powers.

Modern Cryptography: The advent of computers and the digital age brought about a revolution in cryptography. Contemporary cryptographic systems utilise intricate mathematical algorithms and computational methodologies to guarantee the security of digital communications. Public-key cryptography, introduced by Whitfield Diffie and Martin Hellman in the 1970s, revolutionized the field by allowing for secure communication over insecure channels without the need for a shared secret key. The development of encryption standards such as the Data Encryption Standard (DES) and its successor, the Advanced Encryption Standard (AES), further cemented the importance of cryptography in modern computing.

Contemporary Challenges: In the age of the internet and ubiquitous digital communication, Encryption is essential for preserving privacy, securing sensitive information, and guaranteeing the safety of online transactions. Nevertheless, it also poses difficulties for law enforcement and national security authorities endeavouring to combat cybercrime and terrorism while simultaneously considering individual rights to privacy.

The historical development of encryption reflects the evolution of human communication and the perpetual cat-and-mouse game between cryptographers and cryptanalysts striving for security and secrecy in an increasingly interconnected world.

1.2.3 Importance of Encryption

Encryption is crucial for protecting sensitive information and preserving the security and privacy of digital communication and data storage. Its importance can be understood through various key points:

Data Security: Encryption protects data from unauthorized access, ensuring that only authorized users with the decryption key can access the information. This is crucial for safeguarding personal, financial, and sensitive business data.

Privacy Protection: Encryption helps individuals and organizations maintain their privacy by encrypting communications and data. This prevents interception or eavesdropping by malicious actors, governments, or unauthorized third parties.

Compliance Requirements: Many industries and jurisdictions have regulatory requirements mandating the protection of sensitive data through encryption. Compliance with these regulations is essential for avoiding penalties and maintaining trust with customers.

Preventing Data Breaches: The danger of data breaches and illegal access is decreased when data is encrypted both in transit and at rest. Security issues are lessened since even if hackers get to access encrypted data, they will be unable to decrypt it without the decryption key.

Securing Online Transactions: Encrypted systems such as (Secure Sockets Layer/Transport Layer Security) encrypt data exchanged between web browsers and servers, ensuring the confidentiality and integrity of online transactions, including e-commerce and banking.

Protecting Intellectual Property: Encryption helps protect intellectual property by securing confidential documents, proprietary algorithms, and trade secrets. This is vital for businesses seeking to maintain a competitive advantage and preserve their innovations.

Preventing Identity Theft: Encryption helps prevent identity theft by securing personally identifiable information (PII) such as social security numbers, passwords, and financial credentials. This mitigates the risk of identity theft and fraud.

Preserving Confidentiality in Communication: Encrypted communication channels, such as encrypted email and messaging apps, ensure that conversations remain private and immune to interception or surveillance. This is crucial for protecting sensitive discussions in both personal and professional contexts.

Cybersecurity Resilience: Encryption enhances overall cybersecurity resilience by adding an extra layer of defense against cyber threats. It enhances the effectiveness of additional security measures like firewalls, antivirus software, and intrusion detection systems, hence increasing the difficulty for attackers to breach systems and networks.

In summary, encryption is essential for maintaining the confidentiality, integrity, and authenticity of data and communications in an increasingly interconnected and digitized world. Its widespread adoption is critical for protecting critical information and maintaining confidence in digital interactions.

References

- Agarwal, U., Rishiwal, V., Tanwar, S., & Yadav, M. (2024). Blockchain and crypto forensics: Investigating crypto frauds. *International Journal of Network Management, 34*(2), e2255.
- Alam, I. (2024). Information and Communication Technology Cryptography.
- Albaaji, G. F., & Chandra, S. V. (2024). Blockchain technology in agriculture: Digitizing the Iraqi agricultural environment. *Environment, Development and Sustainability*, 1-12.
- Al-Ghuraybi, H. A., AlZain, M. A., & Soh, B. (2024). Exploring the integration of Blockchain technology, physical unclonable function, and machine learning for authentication in cyber-physical systems. *Multimedia Tools and Applications, 83*(12), 35629-35672.
- Alsharari, R. H., Hamdi, H., Aziz, A. A. A. A., & Mahmood, M. A. (2024). Enhancing Security Decision-Making to Prevent Network Attacks Using Blockchain Technology. *International Journal of Intelligent Systems and Applications in Engineering, 12*(8s), 414-425.
- Bhurgri, S. S., Ali, N. I., Korejo, I. A., & Brohi, I. A. (2024). Enhancing Security and Confidentiality in Decentralized Payment System Based on Blockchain Technology. *The Asian Bulletin of Big Data Management, 4*(1), Science-4.
- Bisht, A., Das, A. K., & Giri, D. (2024). Personal health record storage and sharing using searchable encryption and Blockchain: A comprehensive survey. *Security and Privacy, 7*(2), e351.
- Chanal, P. M., & Kakkasageri, M. S. (2024). Blockchain-based data integrity framework for Internet of Things. *International Journal of Information Security, 23*(1), 519-532.
- Diwan, P., Kashyap, R., & Khandelwal, B. (2024). Blockchain assisted encryption scheme for intellectual share estimation using medical research data. *Concurrency and Computation: Practice and Experience, 36*(2), e7896.
- El Kafhali, S. (2024). Blockchain-Based Electronic Voting System: Significance and Requirements. *Mathematical Problems in Engineering, 2024.*
- Gao, H., Duan, P., Pan, X., Zhang, X., Ye, K., & Zhong, Z. (2024). Blockchain-enabled supervised secure data sharing and delegation scheme in Web3.

0. *Journal of Cloud Computing, 13*(1), 21.

- Jia, W., Xie, T., & Wang, B. (2024). A privacy-preserving scheme with multi-level regulation compliance for Blockchain. *Scientific Reports, 14*(1), 438.
- Judijanto, L., Tubagus, M., Hasibuan, R., Mustajab, D., & Rosid, A. (2024). Integration Of Blockchain Technology in The Financial System: Assessing Its Impact on Efficiency, Security, And Stability of Financial Markets. *International Journal of Economic Literature, 2*(1), 41-53.
- Khalafalla, W., Zhu, W. X., Elkhalil, A., & Elfadul, I. (2024). Efficient access control scheme for heterogeneous signcryption based on Blockchain in VANETs. *Cluster Computing*, 1-21.
- Khan, A. A., & Por, L. Y. (2024). Special Issue on Information Security and Cryptography: The Role of Advanced Digital Technology. *Applied Sciences, 14*(5), 2045.
- Korkuc, C., Aytas Korkmaz, N., Genc, Y., Akkoc, A., Afacan, E., & Yazgan, E. (2024). BLOCKBOX: Blockchain based black box designing and modeling. *Concurrency and Computation: Practice and Experience, 36*(13), e8057.
- Kumar, A., Raheja, D., Rawal, J., & Yadav, A. L. (2024, February). Blockchain-driven System for Authentication and Authorization. In *2024 IEEE International Conference on Computing, Power and Communication Technologies (IC2PCT)* (Vol. 5, pp. 796-801). IEEE.
- Lin, M. B., Pele, D. T., & Ren, R. (2024). Understanding Blockchain Technology. *Available at SSRN 4804484.*
- Liu, J., & Wu, J. (2024). A Comprehensive Survey on Blockchain Technology and Its Applications. *Highlights in Science, Engineering and Technology, 85*, 128-138.
- Lizama, M. G., Huesa, J., & Claudio, B. M. (2024). Use of Blockchain technology for the exchange and secure transmission of medical images in the cloud: Systematic Review with Bibliometric Analysis. *ASEAN Journal of Science and Engineering, 4*(1), 71-92.
- Mesci, A., & Eren, E. (2024). How can Blockchain be Integrated into Autonomous Systems to Ensure Data Integrity and Trustworthiness, and What are the Potential Pitfalls in Decentralized Autonomous System Operations?. *Asian Journal of Research in Computer Science, 17*(2), 1-14.
- Mohammed, N. S., Dawood, O. A., Sagheer, A. M., & Nafea, A. A. (2024). Secure Smart Contract Based on Blockchain to Prevent the Non-Repudiation Phenomenon. *Baghdad Science Journal, 21*(1), 0234-0234.
- Orlando, G. (2024). Exploring Crypto & Blockchain in Finance: Present & Future. *Available at SSRN 4787238.*

- Patil, S. D., Kathole, A. B., Kumbhare, S., & Vhatkar, K. (2024). A Blockchain-Based Approach to Ensuring the Security of Electronic Data. *International Journal of Intelligent Systems and Applications in Engineering, 12*(11s), 649-655.
- Pillai, A. V. (2024). Crypto Technology--Impact on Global Economy. *arXiv preprint arXiv:2403.00018.*
- Settipalli, L., Gangadharan, G. R., & Bellamkonda, S. (2024). An extended lightweight Blockchain based collaborative healthcare system for fraud prevention. *Cluster Computing, 27*(1), 563-573.
- Shakor, M. Y., Khaleel, M. I., Safran, M., Alfarhood, S., & Zhu, M. (2024). Dynamic AES Encryption and Blockchain Key Management: A Novel Solution for Cloud Data Security. *IEEE Access.*
- Shamout, M. D., Das, S., Alazzam, M. B., & Nomani, M. Z. M. (2024, March). Role of data security technology in healthcare in protecting confidential patient information and complying with regulations. In *AIP Conference Proceedings* (Vol. 2816, No. 1). AIP Publishing.
- Shree, S., Zhou, C., & Barati, M. (2024). Data protection in internet of medical things using Blockchain and secret sharing method. *The Journal of Supercomputing, 80*(4), 5108-5135.

- Shree, S., Zhou, C., & Barati, M. (2024). Data protection in internet of medical things using Blockchain and secret sharing method. *The Journal of Supercomputing, 80*(4), 5108-5135.

- Vasani, V., Prateek, K., Amin, R., Maity, S., & Dwivedi, A. D. (2024). Embracing the quantum frontier: Investigating quantum communication, cryptography, applications and future directions. *Journal of Industrial Information Integration*, 100594.
- Vashishth, T. K., Sharma, V., Sharma, K. K., Kumar, B., Chaudhary, S., & Panwar, R. (2024). Intelligent Resource Allocation and Optimization for Industrial Robotics Using AI and Blockchain. In *AI and Blockchain Applications in Industrial Robotics* (pp. 82-110). IGI Global.
- Vatambeti, R., Krishna, E. P., Karthik, M. G., & Damera, V. K. (2024). Securing the medical data using enhanced privacy preserving based Blockchain technology in Internet of Things. *Cluster Computing, 27*(2), 1625-1637.
- Verma, G., & Kanrar, S. (2024). Secure document sharing model based on Blockchain technology and attribute-based encryption. *Multimedia Tools and Applications, 83*(6), 16377-16394.

- Walzade, A. K., & Vikhar, P. A. (2024). Secured Electronic Clinical Unified Record Exchange using Blockchain Ledger and Optimized Cryptography. *International Journal of Intelligent Systems and Applications in Engineering, 12*(12s), 46-59.
- Yuan, S., Yang, W., Tian, X., & Tang, W. (2024). A Blockchain-Based Privacy Preserving Intellectual Property Authentication Method. *Symmetry, 16*(5), 622.
- Zhuk, A. (2024). Crypto-anarchy: a paradigm shift for society and the legal system. *Journal of Computer Virology and Hacking Techniques*, 1-27.

II

Introduction to Blockchain technology

LEARNING OBJECTIVES

- Explain the evolution of blockchain from its inception to the present day
- Assess the effectiveness of blockchain in enhancing security over traditional methods.
- Propose improvements to current blockchain technology to enhance its performance.
- Identify the factors that contribute to the importance of blockchain in digital identity verification.
- Analyze the challenges faced by industries in adopting blockchain technologyBottom of Form

2.0 Introduction to Blockchain Technology

The Blockchain technology has emerged as one of the most transformative innovations of the 21st century, revolutionizing the way we think about data, transactions, and trust. Originally devised for the cryptocurrency Bitcoin, Blockchain has evolved to serve a wide array of applications beyond digital currencies, impacting industries ranging from finance and supply chain management to healthcare and voting systems. At its core, a Blockchain is a decentralized and distributed ledger that records transactions across many computers in such a way that the registered transactions cannot be altered retroactively. This ensures the integrity and security of the data, providing a reliable system of record without the need for a central authority.

2.1 **Definition**

A chain of blocks containing transactions, where each block is linked to the previous one using cryptographic hashes, forming an immutable and transparent ledger.

Satoshi Nakamoto

Blockchain is an incorruptible digital ledger of economic transactions that can be programmed to record not just financial transactions but virtually everything of value.

Don Tapscott and Alex Tapscott

A Blockchain is a decentralized, distributed ledger that consists of a chain of blocks, each containing a set of transactions, and maintained by a consensus algorithm to ensure consistency and trust without the need for a central authority.

Vitalik Buterin

A distributed ledger system that employs a network of computers to achieve a unanimity on the contents of a continuously growing set of records, ensuring transparency, security, and immutability of data.

Arvind Narayanan

2.2 Key Themes/ Characteristics Across Definitions

The notion of Blockchain technology is defined in a comprehensive manner from many viewpoints, with each emphasising its fundamental features. These descriptions succinctly capture the fundamental nature of Blockchain technology as a robust, open, and distributed system for documenting transactions and data.

Decentralization: The concept entails a departure from traditional centralized systems, instead embracing a distributed network where authority and control are dispersed across numerous nodes. The absence of a central authority or intermediary, highlighting the decentralized nature of Blockchain ledgers. Through cryptographic techniques, transactions are securely recorded in a chain of blocks, with each block cryptographically linked to its predecessor, ensuring immutability and transparency. This decentralized database is continuously updated by a peer-to-peer network, where consensus mechanisms play a crucial role in maintaining the integrity of the ledger. By removing the reliance on a single point of control, decentralization fosters trust, transparency, and resilience, making Blockchain technology a ground-breaking innovation with far-reaching implications across various industries.

Immutability: A Blockchain operates as a chain of blocks, with each block linked to the previous one using cryptographic hashes. This linkage forms a foundation of immutable records, where once a transaction is recorded in a block, it cannot be altered or deleted without consensus from the network participants. This incorruptible nature of the Blockchain ensures the integrity and transparency of economic transactions and other valuable data. Through the process of decentralisation, the database is fragmented and spread out throughout an ensemble of computers, resulting in a ledger that is very resilient to any attempts of tampering or manipulation. The fact that every block has a timestamp and refers to the one before it reinforces the ledger's chronological and immutable character. This decentralized approach to maintaining a continuously growing list of records guarantees the immutability of data, reinforcing trust and security without the need for a central authority. Thus, immutability serves as a cornerstone principle of Blockchain technology, underpinning its reliability and utility across various applications.

Transparency: The theme of transparency is central across provided. Blockchain is described as a chain of blocks containing transactions, each linked to the previous one using cryptographic hashes, forming an immutable and transparent ledger. It is portrayed as an incorruptible digital ledger that records economic transactions, programmable to capture virtually everything of value, thus emphasizing its transparency. Furthermore, Blockchain is characterized as a decentralized database maintained by a peer-to-peer network, where each block contains a timestamp and a link to the previous block, ensuring transparency through its ordered and publicly accessible records. Consensus algorithms are highlighted as mechanisms that maintain the transparency of the ledger by ensuring consistency and trust without the need for a central authority. Blockchain technology is depicted as a distributed ledger system that achieves consensus among a network of computers, emphasizing transparency as one of its fundamental principles alongside security and immutability of data.

Security: Cryptographic hashes link blocks, securing the data and preventing fraud. The security theme in Blockchain technology revolves around the core principles of immutability, transparency, and decentralization. Blockchain functions as an unalterable digital record, where transactions are saved in blocks connected using cryptographic hash values, creating an unchangeable sequence. This increases the accuracy and reliability of the data by guaranteeing that once the transaction is logged, it cannot be changed or interfered with. Additionally, the decentralized nature of Blockchain, where a network of computers collectively maintains the ledger, contributes to its security by eliminating single points of failure and reducing the risk of malicious attacks. Through consensus algorithms and peer-to-peer validation protocols, Blockchain ensures that the contents of the ledger are agreed upon by the network, promoting trust and eliminating the need for a central authority. This distributed ledger system fosters transparency, as all participants have access to the same information, while maintaining the confidentiality of individual transactions through cryptographic techniques. Blockchain technology provides a robust framework for securing economic transactions and valuable data, offering a high level of security, transparency, and immutability.

Consensus Mechanisms: Protocols are in place to validate and agree on the transactions to be added to the Blockchain. Consensus mechanisms serve as the backbone of Blockchain technology, ensuring the integrity and trustworthiness of the decentralized ledger. Consensus, according to several definitions, is the process by which a group of nodes on a network decides among themselves as to whether a transaction is genuine and what order to add it to the Blockchain. For the ledger to remain transparent and unchangeable, this agreement is essential. Consensus mechanisms allow decentralised databases to reach consensus with no reliance on a central authority, improving security and reducing the danger of corruption or manipulation. By adhering to predefined protocols and algorithms, such as Proof of Work (PoW) or Proof of Stake (PoS), Blockchain networks validate and confirm transactions, ensuring the reliability and integrity of the entire system. Blockchain technology creates a new paradigm of economic interaction by allowing decentralized networks to reach consensus on the ledger's current state through consensus. This leads to pushless transactions.

2.3 **Historical Background**

The historical background of Blockchain technology traces back to its foundational concepts and the progressive evolution that has shaped its current state. Initially conceptualized as a chain of blocks containing specific information, Blockchain emerged as a revolutionary ledger system characterized by its secure, chronological, and immutable nature.

In 1979, one of the foundational technologies for Blockchain was introduced by computer scientist and mathematician Ralph Merkle. He developed the concept of the Merkle tree, a data structure designed to facilitate the verification of individual records. Merkle described an approach known as tree authentication, which was aimed at improving public key distribution and digital signatures. This innovative method allowed for the efficient and secure validation of data within a hierarchical framework. Merkle's work was significant enough to earn a patent for providing digital signatures, laying the groundwork for the cryptographic principles that underpin modern Blockchain technology. The Merkle tree continues to be an essential element in the protection and authenticity of Blockchain systems, as it facilitates the verification of transactions and the linkage of blocks in a decentralised public ledger.

Chaum's pioneering work didn't stop there; he is also credited with inventing digital cash, laying the groundwork for future developments in digital currency. In 1989, Chaum founded DigiCash, a company aimed at bringing his concepts of secure digital transactions to the market. His early contributions significantly influenced the development of cryptographic protocols and digital payment systems, setting the stage for the emergence of Blockchain technology in the following decade.

In 1991, researchers Stuart Haber and W. Scott Stornetta made a significant contribution to the development of Blockchain technology. Faced with the challenge of creating a practical computational solution for timestamping digital documents to prevent tampering and misdating, the duo pioneered a groundbreaking approach. Leveraging the power of cryptography, they collaborated to design a system that would ensure the integrity and immutability of digital records. Their solution involved storing timestamped documents in a sequential chain of blocks, laying the foundation for what would later become known as Blockchain technology. This early innovation set the stage for the evolution of decentralized ledger systems, marking the beginning of a transformative journey towards secure and transparent digital transactions.

In 1992, the foundational groundwork for what would later become Blockchain technology was laid with the creation of Merkle Trees by Stuart Haber and W. Scott Stornetta. This innovation marked a significant milestone in the quest for secure and efficient data storage and verification. Merkle Trees enabled the aggregation of multiple data records into a single block, forming a secured chain of blocks. This approach offered a novel solution for organizing and storing digital information in a tamper-resistant manner. However, despite its potential, the technology did not see widespread adoption at the time. One of the primary reasons for its limited usage was the lack of a practical implementation framework and infrastructure.

Subsequently, in 2004, the landscape of Blockchain technology underwent a significant shift with the introduction of patents related to this field. These patents, while intended to protect intellectual property, inadvertently hindered the further development and adoption of Blockchain technology by imposing legal constraints on its usage. As a result, the momentum behind the early efforts to utilize Merkle Trees and similar innovations for creating efficient and secure data storage systems slowed down considerably.

Despite its temporary setback, the core principles and concepts introduced by Haber, Stornetta, and others continued to resonate within the tech community. At some point, in 2008, a person or organization going to call themselves "pseudonym Satoshi Nakamoto" published the groundbreaking whitepaper Bitcoin, a peer-to-peer electronic cash The chapter outlined a Blockchain-based decentralized digital money system that sparked a rush of invention and rekindled interest in the area. From this point forward, Blockchain technology evolved rapidly, finding applications beyond cryptocurrency, and gradually gaining recognition as a transformative force across various industries.

In the year 2000, Stefan Konst contributed significantly to the early conceptualization of Blockchain technology with his publication of a theory on cryptographic secured chains, along with proposals for their practical implementation. Konst's work laid foundational ideas for utilizing cryptography to create secure and verifiable chains of data, which would later evolve into the concept of Blockchain. His realization of the possible uses of cryptography to ensure the validity and indestructibility of digital data paved the way for the later development of Blockchain technology. Konst's contributions marked an important milestone in the historical progression towards the creation of decentralized, transparent, and tamper-resistant ledger systems that underpin modern Blockchain networks.

In 2004, the cryptographic activist Hal Finney made a significant contribution to the evolution of Blockchain technology by introducing a system called "Reusable Proof of Work." This invention signaled a turning point in the development of encryption and Blockchain. Finney's system addressed a critical issue known as the Double Spending Problem, which had long been a challenge in digital cash systems. By registering the ownership of tokens on a trusted server, Finney's system addressed this issue by facilitating secure and dependable digital transactions. This development laid the groundwork for the subsequent advancements in Blockchain technology, setting the stage for the decentralized and transparent systems that would emerge in the years to come. Finney's contribution demonstrated the potential of cryptography to revolutionize financial transactions and laid the foundation for the decentralized ledger systems that form the backbone of modern Blockchain technology.

The notion of bitcoin and Blockchain technology were first described in a groundbreaking white paper released in 2008 by an individual or group going by the moniker Satoshi Nakamoto. The foundation for a safe peer-to-peer (P2P) transaction system that functioned without the assistance of dependable middlemen like banks or governments was described in this white paper. Over the years, several ideas and conjectures have been generated by the mystery surrounding Nakamoto's genuine identity. Nakamoto created Blockchain architecture and Bitcoin, which were based on ideas and technology that had been developed during the preceding thirty years. The "chain of blocks" concept, which enabled the insertion of blocks to the ledger without requiring their signature from a reliable third party, was one of Nakamoto's most important breakthroughs.

In 2009, amid the Great Recession when governments were injecting significant amounts of money into the economy, a revolutionary financial innovation emerged: cryptocurrency. Satoshi Nakamoto mined the first Bitcoin block, known as the Genesis block or block 0, which contained 50 bitcoins. This event validated the Blockchain concept, demonstrating its potential as a decentralized and immutable ledger. Nakamoto subsequently released Bitcoin version 0.1 as open-source software on SourceForge, a platform now hosted on GitHub.

When Nakamoto delivered 10 bitcoins to the wallet of Hal Finney in block 170, it was the first transaction ever made on the cryptocurrency. To facilitate development and communication, the Bitcoin-dev channel was created on Internet Relay Chat (IRC), allowing users to trade traditional currency for bitcoins. Additionally, Nakamoto launched the Bitcoin Talk forum, providing a space for community engagement and sharing.

In keeping with the idea that cryptocurrencies would be a finite quantity of money, Mr. Nakamoto created a mechanism that would guarantee that there would never be over twenty-one million bitcoins in circulation. This finite supply mechanism remains a core principle of Bitcoin, distinguishing it from traditional fiat currencies.In 2010, Blockchain technology marked a significant milestone when programmer Laszlo Hanyecz made history on May 22 by paying 10,000 bitcoins for two Papa John's pizzas. Valued at approximately $40 at the time, this transaction, known as "Bitcoin Pizza Day," would be worth over $260 million at today's bitcoin prices, highlighting the dramatic increase in Bitcoin's value over the years.

The following year, the Tokyo-based Bitcoin exchange Mt. Gox was established by programmer Jed McCaleb. Initially designed as a platform for trading Magic: The Gathering cards, Mt. Gox (short for Magic: The Gathering Online eXchange) quickly rose to prominence, becoming the largest Bitcoin exchange globally and handling over 70% of all Bitcoin transactions at its peak. However, in August, a hacker exploited a flaw in the Blockchain code, generating over 184 billion bitcoins in block 74,638. This incident severely damaged Bitcoin's reputation. In response, Bitcoin's creator, Satoshi Nakamoto, released an updated version of the Bitcoin software to fix the vulnerability. By the end of the year, Nakamoto had mysteriously stepped away from the Bitcoin community, leaving the future of the digital currency to its expanding community of developers and enthusiasts.

Significant advancements in Blockchain technology and the cryptocurrency space were accomplished in 2011. By now, twenty-five percent of the twenty million bitcoins had been mined. Early in February, the value of bitcoin was equivalent to the US dollar, demonstrating how widely accepted it is. Soon afterward, Mark Karpelès purchased Mt. Gox from Jed McCaleb. As it rose, the value of bitcoin matched that of the British pound and euro. As bitcoin started to receive donations, WikiLeaks demonstrated how it might be used for cross-border, censorship-resistant transactions. Unfortunately, there was a cyberattack on Mt. Gox, which led to substantial bitcoin theft and a halt of trade. With its inception in October, Litecoin became one of the first alternative cryptocurrencies and added diversity to the market.

Interest in cryptocurrencies solidified in 2012, marking it as a crucial year for Blockchain and the crypto industry. Bitcoin's price fluctuated around $5, and Mihai Alisie and Vitalik Buterin, future founders of Ethereum, launched Bitcoin Magazine, with its first issue in May. The Bitcoin Foundation was also established to promote Bitcoin and restore public trust in cryptocurrencies following several scandals. In the same year, Jed McCaleb and Chris Larsen established OpenCoin, which paved the way for the creation of the Ripple transaction protocol, which facilitates real-time payments and currency exchanges. Furthermore, Coinbase successfully raised over $600,000 in a seed round that was crowdfunded, which helped the company become a well-known Bitcoin exchange. These events collectively strengthened the legitimacy and infrastructure of the cryptocurrency ecosystem.

The year 2013 was notable for Bitcoin's rapid rise, highlighting significant advancements in Blockchain technology. According to Coinbase, $1 million worth of Bitcoin was sold in February at a price of more than $22 apiece. With 11 million Bitcoin in use as of March, the cryptocurrency's entire market value surpassed $1 billion. The first Bitcoin ATM was installed in a Vancouver coffee shop in October, indicating the currency's increasing popularity. But the year was not without its difficulties, as cryptocurrency was outlawed in China and Thailand and Mt. Gox's funds were seized by the US Federal Court for operating without a money transmission authorization. In addition to collecting around 144,000 Bitcoin valued at over $1 billion, the FBI took down the dark web marketplace Silk Road and sentenced its leader, Ross Ulbricht, to life in prison for a number of offenses. Despite these setbacks, 2013 highlighted Blockchain technology's potential and vulnerabilities.

In 2014, Ethereum's creation marked a pivotal moment in Blockchain history. Vitalik Buterin's white paper introduced a decentralized application platform with smart contracts, expanding Blockchain's use beyond cryptocurrency. Financial institutions and various industries began exploring Blockchain's potential, even as Bitcoin's reputation suffered due to incidents like the Mt. Gox bankruptcy. By the end of the year, major companies such as Microsoft and PayPal accepted Bitcoin, demonstrating Blockchain's growing influence.

The Ethereum Ethereum Frontier networks went live in 2015, opening the door for decentralized apps and smart contracts while also drawing a thriving development community. Hyperledger was introduced by the Linux Foundation, and Nasdaq started a Blockchain pilot. To investigate Blockchain's potential applications, nine large banks established the R3 consortium, which in six months grew to include over 40 institutions. Ethereum rose to prominence as a top Blockchain platform quite fast.

The term "Blockchain" has gained widespread acceptance by 2016. In order to promote industry advocacy and education, the Hyperledger project and the Chamber of Digital Commerce joined. A serious flaw in the DAO code of Ethereum caused a hard fork, and the Bitfinex cryptocurrency exchange suffered a breach that resulted in the loss of around 120,000 Bitcoin, or roughly $66 million.

When Bitcoin hit a record high of around $20,000 in 2017, Japan accepted it as legitimate money. The Digital Trade Chain Consortium was established by seven European banks to facilitate Blockchain-based trade finance. About 15% of international banks employed Blockchain technology in some form. Block.one launched the EOS Blockchain operating system for decentralized applications.

2018 saw a roughly $3,800 decline in the value of Bitcoin, and big websites including Stripe, Google, Twitter, and Facebook blocked users from using cryptocurrencies. South Korea pledged to make large Blockchain investment while outlawing anonymous cryptocurrency trading. In an effort to encourage Blockchain development, the European Commission formed the Blockchain Observatory and Forum, and Baidu unveiled its Blockchain-as-a-service platform.Significant advancements in Blockchain technology were made in 2019. Walmart introduced a supply chain system built on Hyperledger. Amazon rolled out Amazon Managed Blockchain, aiding in Web 3.0 app development. Ethereum surpassed one million daily transactions. Organizations embraced Blockchain for diverse applications, highlighting its growing importance in sectors like supply chain management and decentralized applications. This year marked a pivotal moment in Blockchain's evolution, signaling its potential to revolutionize various industries.

According to a Deloitte report, Blockchain technology gained significant traction in 2020, with over 40% of organizations incorporating it into production and 55% ranking it as a high strategic goal. Ethereum 2.0 was established with the introduction of the Beacon Chain. Because they provided stability in contrast to erratic cryptocurrencies, stablecoins gained popularity. This was a turning point in the development of the technology, with more interest being shown in combining Blockchain with AI for commercial optimization.

In 2021, Blockchain technology witnessed remarkable growth beyond cryptocurrency. Bitcoin soared to a record high, reaching $68,789.63, with its market cap surpassing $3 trillion. Coinbase's IPO marked a significant milestone, while the DeFi market expanded by 600%, hitting $200 billion. NFT art sales, like one at Christie's for over $69 million in Ethereum, made headlines. Entrepreneurs like Elon Musk embraced crypto payments, fueling broader Blockchain adoption. Governments and enterprises explored Blockchain for diverse applications, from voting to vaccine distribution amid the pandemic. Cloud providers offered Blockchain services, reflecting escalating demand for Blockchain talent. The market, valued at nearly $6 billion, was projected to exceed a trillion dollars by 2030, as per Statista.

In 2022, Blockchain technology saw both milestones and challenges. NFTs surged, eco-friendly networks emerged, and corporate Blockchain adoption grew. Bitcoin mining neared its 21-million-coin limit, heightening scarcity. However, cryptocurrency prices plummeted amid inflation fears and the Omicron variant, causing exchange bankruptcies. Regulatory uncertainty loomed, yet promised legitimacy. Major setbacks included collapses of platforms like FTX and Terra. Hacks plagued the industry, with losses totaling $3.8 billion, underscoring the need for enhanced security measures.

Despite regulatory challenges and cryptocurrency controversies, Blockchain technology persists, albeit with increased scrutiny. Originally tied to finance, its applications now span industries like gaming, healthcare, and supply chain management. With Web 3.0 promising decentralization and data security, Blockchain's potential expands. Bitcoin stabilizes in the range of $25,000 toward $30,000, as its withdrawal steadily approaches the 21 million limit set by Satoshi Nakamoto, expected to be reached around the year 2140.

Blockchain technology has evolved rapidly beyond 2023, promising secure and transparent transactions, disrupting traditional business operations across industries. With projections by Gartner estimating its business value at over $360 billion by 2026 and potentially surpassing $3.1 trillion by 2030, Blockchain's impact is profound. Key trends driving its growth include its role in digital transformation initiatives, synergy with AI for enhanced efficiency, and the "rise of non-fungible tokens (NFTs)" for new revenue streams. Additionally, Blockchain's integration with Internet of Things (IoT) devices ensures faster, more secure digital transactions, while smart contracts streamline processes. Blockchain's significance extends to Web 3.0 and the metaverse, underpinning decentralized finance (DeFi) and Blockchain-as-a-service solutions. The proof-of-stake protocol gains traction for its energy efficiency, while governments increasingly adopt distributed ledger technology for improved governance. Despite regulatory challenges and security concerns, Blockchain's expansion is fueled by ongoing research and investment, driving advancements in security, privacy, scalability, and interoperability. As businesses navigate Blockchain deployments, careful consideration of risks and costs remains crucial in harnessing its transformative potential.

2.4 Importance of Blockchain

Blockchain technology has a profound impact on traditional systems and processes, revolutionising them in profound ways. Its significance is felt across a variety of sectors and aspects of contemporary society. Here are some key points highlighting its significance:

Decentralization and Trust: Blockchain technology eliminates the need for intermediaries by enabling peer-to-peer transactions, thus reducing costs and delays associated with traditional centralized systems. Decentralization enhances user trust by transparently and immutably recording transactions on the Blockchain. This ensures data integrity and minimizes the potential for fraud or manipulation.

Enhanced Security: The cryptographic techniques employed in Blockchain ensure the security of transactions and data, making them resistant to tampering and unauthorized access. Each block is linked to the previous one using cryptographic hashes, creating a chain of blocks that is highly secure and virtually immutable. This heightened security makes Blockchain technology particularly valuable for applications involving sensitive data, such as financial transactions, healthcare records, and identity management.

Transparency and Accountability: Through the maintenance of an easily available and verifiable record of transactions, Blockchain technology allows players to keep an eye on the history of assets and validate their legitimacy. Transparency fosters integrity and reduces the possibility of corruption or manipulation, especially in areas where disclosure is crucial, such voting procedures, supply chain management, and government operations.

Efficiency and Cost Reduction: By automating processes and eliminating the need for intermediaries, Blockchain technology streamlines operations and reduces administrative costs. Enabling automated and efficient transactions, smart contracts operate as self-executing protocols that have specific requirements embedded into the Blockchain. This further reduces the necessity for manual intervention and documentation.

Innovation and Disruption: A surge of innovation has been sparked across industries by Blockchain technology, which has unlocked new opportunities for business models, products, as well as services. From decentralized finance (DeFi) and tokenization of assets to decentralized applications (DApps) and non-fungible tokens (NFTs), Blockchain has opened up avenues for creativity and disruption, challenging traditional paradigms and empowering individuals and organizations to innovate and create value in unprecedented ways.

Financial Inclusion: Blockchain technology holds the promise of broadening access to financial services for underserved communities, thereby fostering greater financial inclusion and empowerment. Through decentralized finance (DeFi) platforms and digital currencies, Blockchain technology can provide access to banking, lending, and investment opportunities to individuals who lack access to traditional financial services, thereby promoting economic empowerment and social equity.

2.5 Scope of Blockchain technology across industries

The scope of Blockchain technology spans across various industries, revolutionizing traditional business processes and enabling new possibilities for efficiency, transparency, and security. Here's an overview of how Blockchain is transforming different sectors:

2.5.1 Finance and Banking:

The scope of Blockchain technology in finance and banking is vast, revolutionizing traditional banking processes and offering innovative solutions to longstanding challenges. Here's a detailed explanation of its scope in this sector:

A. Payment Processing:

Cross-Border Payments: Blockchain enables near-instantaneous cross-border transactions at reduced costs compared to traditional methods, bypassing intermediaries like correspondent banks.

Remittances: Blockchain-powered remittance services offer cheaper and faster alternatives for sending money across borders, particularly beneficial for individuals in underserved regions.

Micropayments: Blockchain facilitates low-cost micropayments, enabling new business models and revenue streams for content creators and service providers.

B. Smart Contracts:

Automated Settlements: Smart contracts automate contract execution and settlement processes, reducing the need for manual intervention and eliminating the risk of fraud or error.

Trade Finance: Smart contracts streamline trade finance processes by automating letter of credit issuance, trade documentation, and payment settlements, reducing paperwork and delays.

Loan Origination: Blockchain-based smart contracts enable automated loan origination processes, including borrower verification, collateral management, and loan disbursement, enhancing efficiency and reducing operational costs.

C. Identity Verification:

KYC Compliance: Blockchain facilitates secure and efficient Know Your Customer (KYC) processes by enabling the sharing of verified identity information across financial institutions while ensuring user privacy and data protection.

Digital Identity: Blockchain enables individuals to maintain self-sovereign digital identities, giving them control over their personal information and reducing the risk of identity theft and fraud.

Authentication: Blockchain-based authentication systems provide secure and tamper-proof verification of user identities, enhancing security and trust in online transactions and interactions.

D. Asset Tokenization:

Tokenized Securities: Blockchain enables the issuance, trading, and settlement of tokenized securities, such as stocks, bonds, and derivatives, on decentralized exchanges, improving liquidity and accessibility for investors.

Real Estate Tokenization: Blockchain enables the division of ownership and exchange of real estate assets into smaller units using tokenization, allowing investors to diversify their portfolios and access previously illiquid assets.

Commodities Trading: Blockchain-powered platforms enable the digitization and trading of commodities, such as precious metals and agricultural products, reducing counterparty risk and improving market efficiency.

E. Regulatory Compliance:

Transaction Transparency: A clear and irrevocable account of financial transactions is provided by Blockchain technology, enhancing regulatory compliance and auditability for financial institutions.

AML and CFT Compliance: Blockchain-based solutions enable more effective anti-money laundering (AML) and counter-terrorism financing (CFT) compliance by providing enhanced transaction monitoring and reporting capabilities.

Regulatory Reporting: Blockchain streamlines regulatory reporting processes by automating data collection and verification, reducing the administrative burden on financial institutions and regulators.

F. Central Bank Digital Currencies (CBDCs):

Digital Payment Infrastructure: CBDCs built on Blockchain technology offer central banks a secure and efficient infrastructure for issuing and managing digital currencies, facilitating faster and cheaper payments.

Financial Inclusion: CBDCs can improve financial inclusion by providing unbanked and underbanked populations with access to digital payment services and financial products, reducing reliance on cash-based transactions.

Monetary Policy Tools: CBDCs enable central banks to implement monetary policy more effectively by providing real-time data on economic transactions and facilitating targeted interventions, such as stimulus payments and interest rate adjustments.

The Blockchain technology has the potential to transform finance and banking by enhancing efficiency, reducing costs, improving security, and expanding financial inclusion. As the technology continues to mature and regulatory frameworks evolve, its impact on the sector is expected to grow significantly in the coming years.

2.5.2. Supply Chain Management

The scope of Blockchain technology in supply chain management is vast, offering significant benefits in terms of transparency, traceability, efficiency, and security throughout the entire supply chain ecosystem. Here's a detailed explanation of its scope:

A. **Traceability**

   a. Product Provenance
   b. Anti-Counterfeiting

B. **Transparency**

   a. Real-Time Visibility
   b. Supplier Accountability

C. **Efficiency**

   a. Streamlined Processes
   b. Faster Settlements

D. **Security**

a. Data Integrity
b. Cybersecurity

E. **Risk Management**

a. Predictive Analytics
b. Contingency Planning

F. **Compliance and Sustainability**

a. Regulatory Compliance

A. **Traceability:**

Product Provenance: Blockchain enables the recording of each stage in a product, from raw materials to finished goods. This provides stakeholders and consumers with transparent and immutable information about the origin, manufacturing processes, and handling of products.

Anti-Counterfeiting: By tracking products on the Blockchain, it becomes easier to verify their authenticity and identify counterfeit items. This helps in protecting brand reputation and ensuring consumer safety.

B. Transparency:

Real-Time Visibility: Blockchain facilitates real-time tracking of goods as they move through the supply chain, allowing stakeholders to monitor inventory levels, shipment statuses, and delivery schedules accurately.

Supplier Accountability: Blockchain technology enables all stakeholders in the supply chain to view and verify data about suppliers' performance, thereby guaranteeing adherence to ethical and regulatory standards.

C. Efficiency:

Streamlined Processes: Blockchain streamlines supply chain processes by automating documentation, reducing paperwork, and eliminating manual errors. Smart contracts can automate transactions and trigger actions based on predefined conditions, such as delivery milestones or quality checks.

Faster Settlements: By automating payment processes and reducing the necessity for middlemen, such as banking institutions or processors of payments, Blockchain facilitates transparent and expedited settlements between trading partners.

D. Security:

Data Integrity: Blockchain's decentralized and tamper-proof nature ensures the integrity of supply chain data, making it resistant to tampering, fraud, and unauthorized modifications. Each transaction recorded on the Blockchain is cryptographically linked to previous transactions, creating an immutable audit trail.

Cybersecurity: By decentralizing data storage and utilizing cryptographic techniques, Blockchain enhances cybersecurity in supply chains, minimising the likelihood of unauthorised exposure of confidential data and information breaches.

E. Risk Management:

Predictive Analytics: Blockchain data, combined with advanced analytics and AI, can provide valuable insights into supply chain trends, risks, and potential disruptions. This enables proactive risk management and mitigation strategies.

Contingency Planning: With Blockchain, supply chain stakeholders can identify potential bottlenecks or points of failure in advance and develop contingency plans to minimize the impact of disruptions, such as natural disasters or geopolitical events.

F. Compliance and Sustainability:

Regulatory Compliance: Blockchain facilitates compliance with regulatory requirements by providing transparent and auditable records of transactions and processes. This is particularly beneficial in industries with stringent regulations, such as food and pharmaceuticals.

Sustainability Tracking: Blockchain enables the tracking of environmental and social impact metrics throughout the supply chain, allowing companies to monitor and improve their sustainability practices, such as reducing carbon emissions or ensuring fair labor practices.

Blockchain technology can transmute the management of supply chains by improving openness, effectiveness, safety, and sustainability throughout the entire supply chain ecosystem, from the sourcing of raw materials to the delivery of goods to the final consumer.

2.5.3. Healthcare:

The scope of Blockchain technology in healthcare is vast, offering numerous opportunities to address longstanding challenges and revolutionize the way healthcare data is managed, shared, and utilized. Here's an explanation of the scope of Blockchain in healthcare:

A. Patient Data Management:

Interoperability: Blockchain can facilitate seamless and secure sharing of patient data across healthcare providers, improving coordination of care and patient outcomes.

Data Integrity: By recording patient data on an immutable ledger, Blockchain ensures the integrity and authenticity of medical records, reducing the risk of data breaches and fraud.

Patient-Controlled Access: Patients can have greater control over their own medical records, granting permission for specific healthcare providers or researchers to access their data securely.

B. Drug Traceability and Supply Chain Management:

Counterfeit Prevention: Blockchain enables the tracking of pharmaceuticals throughout the supply chain, Minimising the distribution of fraudulent medications and guaranteeing the well-being of patients.

Transparency: Stakeholders can have continuous insight into the movement of drugs, guaranteeing compliance with regulations and ethical standards.

C. Clinical Trials and Research:

Data Integrity: Blockchain can enhance the integrity and transparency of clinical trial data by recording trial protocols, participant consent, and results on an immutable ledger.

Patient Recruitment: Smart contracts can automate the recruitment process for clinical trials, matching eligible participants with researchers while ensuring privacy and consent.

D. Healthcare Payments and Billing:

Streamlined Transactions: Blockchain-based systems can facilitate secure and efficient healthcare payments, reducing administrative costs and processing times.

Fraud Prevention: Blockchain enhances transparency in billing processes, reducing the risk of fraudulent claims and billing errors.

E. Identity Management and Authentication:

Patient Identification: Blockchain offers a robust and unalterable approach to ensure security and prevent tampering when verifying patient identities, reducing instances of medical identity theft, and ensuring accurate patient matching.

Credentialing: Healthcare professionals' credentials, licenses, and certifications can be securely recorded on the Blockchain, streamlining the credentialing process and ensuring compliance with regulatory requirements.

F. Medical Research and Data Sharing:

Data Privacy: Blockchain facilitates secure and privacy-preserving data sharing among researchers, enabling collaborative research efforts while protecting patient data privacy.

Incentivized Data Sharing: Patients and healthcare providers can be incentivized to contribute anonymized data to research initiatives through Blockchain-based token economies.

G. Healthcare IoT and Wearables:

Data Security: Blockchain guarantees the confidentiality and accuracy of data produced by IoT devices and wearables, enabling safe transmission and storage of sensitive health data.

Interoperability: Blockchain can enable interoperability among diverse healthcare IoT devices and platforms, creating a unified ecosystem for managing and analyzing health data.

H. Telemedicine and Remote Patient Monitoring:

Data Accessibility: Blockchain facilitates secure access to remote patient monitoring data for healthcare providers, improving remote care delivery and patient outcomes.

Smart Contracts: Automated smart contracts can streamline payments and reimbursement processes for telemedicine services, enhancing efficiency and transparency.

Blockchain technology holds immense promise for transforming healthcare by addressing issues related to data management, interoperability, security, and patient privacy. By leveraging Blockchain-based solutions, the healthcare industry can usher in a new era of transparency, efficiency, and patient-centric care delivery.

2.5.4. Real Estate:

The scope of Blockchain technology in real estate is substantial, offering transformative solutions to longstanding challenges within the industry. Here's an overview of how Blockchain is impacting the real estate sector:

A.**Property Ownership and Title Management:** Transparent Transactions: Blockchain facilitates the clear and unchangeable documentation of property ownership changes, hence decreasing instances of fraud and disputes.

Digital Titles: Digitizing property titles and recording ownership changes on the Blockchain streamlines the title transfer process, making it more efficient and secure.

Smart Contracts: Smart contracts automate and enforce property transactions, ensuring compliance with predefined terms and conditions without the need for intermediaries.

B.**Real Estate Investment:**

Fractional Ownership: Blockchain allows for the fractionalization of real estate assets, enabling investors to purchase and trade fractional shares of properties.

Tokenization: Real estate assets can be tokenized and represented as digital tokens on the Blockchain, facilitating liquidity and enabling broader participation in real estate markets.

Global Access: Blockchain offers a limitless platform for real estate investment, facilitating investors from various geographical locations to effortlessly access and participate in property investments.

Property Management:

Immutable Records: Property management activities such as leasing agreements, rental payments, and maintenance records can be securely recorded on the Blockchain, ensuring transparency and accountability.

Automated Processes: Smart contracts automate property management tasks, such as rent collection and maintenance scheduling, reducing administrative overhead and human error.

Tenant Verification: Blockchain-based identity verification solutions enhance the screening and verification of tenants, improving security and reducing the risk of rental fraud.

C.**Crowdfunding and Financing:**

Access to Capital: Blockchain-powered crowdfunding platforms allow real estate developers to acquire funds from an international network of investors, democratizing access to real estate investment opportunities.

Lower Costs: By eliminating intermediaries and reducing administrative overhead, Blockchain-based financing solutions lower the costs associated with real estate crowdfunding and financing.

Fractionalized Ownership: Fractional ownership of real estate assets through Blockchain tokenization enables smaller investors to engage in massive real estate ventures that were previously out of reach.

D.**Property Records and Compliance:**

Tamper-Proof Records: Property records savedd on the Blockchain are inert and impervious to modification, ensuring the integrity and authenticity of ownership records.

Regulatory Compliance: Blockchain technology can automate compliance processes related to property transactions, such as property taxes, zoning regulations, and land use restrictions, reducing compliance risks and administrative burdens.

Auditable Transactions: Blockchain provides an auditable trail of property transactions, facilitating regulatory audits and ensuring compliance with legal requirements.

E.**Cross-Border Transactions:**

Global Transactions: Blockchain facilitates smooth and effective international real estate transactions by eliminating the requirement for intermediaries and decreasing transaction expenses.

Instant Settlement: Blockchain-powered payment solutions facilitate immediate settlement of real estate transactions, thereby diminishing the time and expenses linked to conventional payment methods.

Legal Clarity: All parties involved can benefit from legal clarity and certainty as smart contracts on the Blockchain automate the implementation and enforcement of cross-border real estate transactions.

The Blockchain technology holds immense potential to revolutionize the real estate industry by enhancing transparency, efficiency, and accessibility in property transactions, investment, and management. As the technology continues to mature, its adoption in real estate is expected to increase, unlocking new opportunities and transforming traditional practices in the sector.

2.5.5. Government and Public Sector: The scope of Blockchain technology in the government and public sector is vast, offering numerous opportunities to enhance transparency, efficiency, and trust in various administrative processes. Here's an overview of how Blockchain is transforming this sector:

A. Identity Management:

Secure Identity Verification: Blockchain-based identity management systems can provide citizens with secure and tamper-proof digital identities, reducing the risk of identity theft and fraud.

Streamlined Services: Governments can use Blockchain to streamline the delivery of public services by securely verifying citizen identities and reducing paperwork.

B. Voting Systems:

Transparent and Secure Elections: Blockchain-based voting platforms can protect the credibility and transparency of electoral processes, reducing the risk of fraud and manipulation.

Remote and Secure Voting: Blockchain technology enables citizens to securely cast their votes from anywhere, increasing voter accessibility and participation.

C. Supply Chain Management:

Transparency and Accountability: Blockchain technology can be employed by governments to monitor the transportation of commodities and services across supply chains, ensuring transparency and accountability.

Preventing Counterfeiting: Blockchain technology can help governments combat counterfeiting by providing a transparent record of product provenance and authenticity.

D. Public Finance and Budgeting:

Transparent Budget Allocation: Blockchain-based systems can provide transparent and immutable records of government spending, allowing citizens o monitor the allocation and utilisation of public cash.

Reducing Corruption: By increasing transparency and accountability in financial transactions, Blockchain can help governments reduce corruption and ensure the proper use of public funds.

E. Land Registry and Property Management:

Secure Property Records: Governments can use Blockchain to create tamper-proof land registries and property records, reducing disputes over land ownership and improving land management.

Efficient Title Transfers: Blockchain technology has the potential to simplify the process of transferring property titles by offering safe and accessible records of ownership transactions.

F. Healthcare Records Management:

Secure and Interoperable Health Records: Blockchain solutions can facilitate the secure and seamless interchange of healthcare records among health care professionals, improving patient care and reducing administrative burdens.

Patient Consent Management: Blockchain can create an easily accessible and auditable database of patient consent for sharing medical data, ensuring compliance with privacy regulations.

G. Taxation and Revenue Collection:

Transparent Taxation: Governments can use Blockchain to create transparent and immutable records of tax payments and revenue collection, reducing tax evasion and fraud.

Efficient Revenue Distribution: Blockchain-based systems can streamline the distribution of government benefits and subsidies by ensuring transparent and accountable allocation of funds.

H. Public Safety and Law Enforcement:

Secure and Immutable Evidence Management: Law enforcement organisations can use Blockchain technology to create safe and impermeable recordings of evidence, preserving the validity of criminal investigations.

Identity Verification for Public Safety: Blockchain-based identity management systems can help law enforcement agencies verify the identity of individuals, enhancing public safety and security.

By leveraging Blockchain technology, governments and public sector organizations can improve transparency, efficiency, and trust in their operations, ultimately leading to better service delivery and enhanced citizen satisfaction. However, adoption of Blockchain in these sectors requires careful consideration of regulatory, privacy, and security concerns.

2.5.6. Energy Sector:

The scope of Blockchain technology in the energy sector is vast, offering numerous opportunities for innovation and efficiency improvements. Here's an exploration of how Blockchain can transform the energy industry:

A.Decentralized Energy Grids: Blockchain can help in the move to decentralised energy networks by enabling peer-to-peer energy trading. Consumers can buy and sell excess energy directly with their neighbours, reducing reliance on centralized utilities and optimizing energy distribution.

B.Real-Time Data Management: Blockchain's ability to securely record and timestamp transactions can enhance grid management by providing real-time visibility into energy production, consumption, and storage. This enables more accurate forecasting and optimization of energy resources.

C. Renewable Energy Integration:

Renewable Energy Certificates (RECs): Blockchain can streamline the issuance, tracking, and trading of Renewable Energy Certificates, which certify the production of renewable energy. This ensures transparency and integrity in renewable energy markets, incentivizing investment in clean energy sources.

Peer-to-Peer Renewable Energy Trading: Blockchain enables direct trading of surplus energy generated from renewable sources between producers and consumers. This promotes the adoption of distributed renewable energy generation and reduces reliance on traditional fossil fuel-based power plants.

D. Energy Supply Chain Management:

Traceability of Energy Sources: Blockchain can track the origin and movement of energy throughout the supply chain, guaranteeing Responsibility and openness. This is especially useful for determining the veracity of green energy claims and lowering the danger of fraud in energy trading.

Efficiency in Energy Transactions: Smart contracts powered by Blockchain technology can automate energy transactions and settlements, reducing administrative overhead and minimizing errors. This improves the efficiency of energy trading and billing processes.

E. Demand Response and Energy Efficiency:

Smart Grids and IoT Integration: Blockchain can integrate with IoT devices and smart meters to allow for immediate tracking and administration of the use of energy. This lets for dynamic demand response programs, where energy users adjust their consumption patterns in response to price signals or grid conditions.

Incentive Mechanisms: Blockchain-based incentive programs, such as tokenized rewards for energy conservation or peak shaving, can encourage consumers to adopt energy-efficient practices and reduce overall energy demand.

F. Carbon Emissions Trading:

Carbon Credits and Offset Markets: Blockchain can enhance the transparency and integrity of carbon emissions trading by securely recording carbon credits on a decentralized ledger. This ensures that carbon offsets are accurately accounted for and verified, facilitating compliance with emissions reduction targets.

Automated Emissions Reporting: Smart contracts can automate the reporting and verification of carbon emissions data, reducing administrative burdens and improving the accuracy of emissions tracking. This enables more efficient management of carbon reduction initiatives.

G. Energy Access and Microgrids:

Decentralized Energy Access: Blockchain-powered microgrids can provide reliable and affordable energy access to remote or underserved communities. By enabling collaborative energy trading and decentralized governance, Blockchain authorizes local communities to manage their energy resources autonomously.

Off-Grid Solutions: Blockchain can support off-grid energy solutions, such as solar-powered microgrids, by facilitating secure payments and transactions in areas with limited access to traditional banking infrastructure.

Blockchain technology has the potential to revolutionize the energy sector by promoting decentralization, transparency, and efficiency. By leveraging Blockchain solutions, the energy industry can accelerate the transition towards renewable energy, optimize grid operations, and empower consumers to actively participate in the energy market.

2.5.7. Entertainment and Media:

The scope of Blockchain technology in the entertainment and media industry is vast and offers numerous opportunities for innovation and transformation. Here's an overview of how Blockchain is impacting this sector:

A. Content Distribution:

Decentralized Platforms: Blockchain enables the creation of decentralized content distribution platforms where artists and content creators can directly connect with consumers without intermediaries. This lowers distribution costs and enables innovators to keep a larger portion of earnings.

Royalty Tracking: Smart contracts on the Blockchain can automate royalty payments to artists and content creators based on predetermined terms, ensuring transparency and fair compensation for their work ***Digital Rights Management (DRM):*** Blockchain-based DRM solutions provide secure and tamper-proof management of digital rights, preventing unauthorized distribution and piracy of content.

B. Intellectual Property Protection:

Content Ownership: Blockchain technology has the capability to timestamp and securely record ownership of intellectual property rights, encompassing various forms of digital content such as music, films, and other media. This ensures proof of ownership and helps prevent plagiarism and unauthorized use of content.

Content Authentication: Blockchain-based authentication systems can verify the authenticity of digital content, including artwork, photographs, and audiovisual materials, by creating immutable records of their creation and ownership history.

C. Micropayments and Content Monetization:

Tokenization: Content creators can tokenize their work on the Blockchain, allowing fans and consumers to purchase and trade digital assets representing ownership or access rights to content. This opens up new revenue streams for creators and enables micropayments for individual pieces of content or specific actions, such as liking or sharing.

Fan Engagement: Blockchain-powered platforms can facilitate direct interactions between content creators and their fans, allowing fans to support their favorite artists through microtransactions, crowdfunding campaigns, and exclusive content subscriptions.

D. Ticketing and Events Management:

Fraud Prevention: Blockchain-based ticketing systems can prevent ticket fraud and scalping by creating secure and traceable tickets that are linked to individual identities or digital wallets. This ensures that tickets cannot be counterfeited or resold at inflated prices.

Transparency: Blockchain technology provides transparency in event ticket sales by recording transactions on a public ledger, allowing organizers to track ticket sales in real-time and ensure fair distribution of tickets.

E. Data Privacy and Security:

User Control: Blockchain-based platforms give users greater control over their personal data by allowing them to decide how their data is shared and used. Users can grant permission to access their data to trusted parties, such as content providers or advertisers, while maintaining privacy and security.

Anti-Piracy Measures: Blockchain technology enables the creation of digital watermarks or fingerprints for content, facilitating the tracking and identification of instances of infringement. This feature assists those who create content and possess the rights to it in safeguarding their intellectual property and ensuring the implementation of copyright regulations.

F. Collaborative Content Creation:

Smart Contracts: Smart contracts on the Blockchain can automate the process of collaboration and revenue sharing among multiple creators, such as musicians, filmmakers, and writers. This makes sure that everyone who helped make the content is paid fairly according to rules that have already been set.

Decentralized Production: Blockchain-based platforms make it possible for content to be produced and distributed without a central authority. This means that artists from all over the world can work together on projects with no need for studios or production companies.

Blockchain technology has the potential to revolutionize the entertainment and media industry by empowering creators, protecting intellectual property rights, and enhancing transparency and trust in content distribution and consumption. As the adoption of Blockchain keeps increasing, more disruptive developments and innovations within this fast-paced industry are likely to come.

Blockchain technology represents a paradigm shift in how data is managed and transactions are conducted. Its decentralized nature, coupled with enhanced security and transparency, offers numerous benefits across various sectors. As the technology continues to evolve, it holds the potential to transform industries, driving innovation and fostering trust in digital interactions. Gaining a comprehensive understanding of the basic principles of Blockchain is crucial for anybody seeking to effectively navigate and exploit the potential advantages offered by this revolutionary technology.

References

- Addula, S. R., Meduri, K., Nadella, G. S., & Gonaygunta, H. AI, and Blockchain in Finance: Opportunities and Challenges for the Banking Sector.
- Aktas, D. (2024). Blockchain Application in Government. *Exploring Blockchain Applications: Management Perspectives.*
- Ali, V., Norman, A. A., & Azzuhri, S. R. B. (2023). Characteristics of Blockchain and its relationship with trust. *IEEE Access, 11*, 15364-15374.
- Al-Mohamad, S., Khaki, A. R., & Sraieb, M. (2024). Cryptocurrency and Real Estate Transactions. In *Blockchain in Real Estate: Theoretical Advances and New Empirical Applications* (pp. 103-122). Singapore: Springer Nature Singapore.
- Andreoulaki, I., Papapostolou, A., & Marinakis, V. (2024). Evaluating the Barriers to Blockchain Adoption in the Energy Sector: A Multicriteria Approach Using the Analytical Hierarchy Process for Group Decision Making. *Energies, 17*(6), 1278.
- Behl, A., Jayawardena, N. S., Pereira, V., & Sampat, B. (2024). Assessing retailer readiness to use Blockchain technology to improve supply chain performance. *Journal of Enterprise Information Management, 37*(2), 673-697.
- Bennet, D., Maria, L., Sanjaya, Y. P. A., & Zahra, A. R. A. (2024). Blockchain technology: Revolutionizing transactions in the digital age. *ADI Journal*

on Recent Innovation, 5(2), 192-199.

- Castellon, C., Roy, S., Kreidl, P., Dutta, A., & Bölöni, L. (2021, October). Energy efficient merkle trees for Blockchains. In *2021 IEEE 20th International Conference on Trust, Security and Privacy in Computing and Communications (TrustCom)* (pp. 1093-1099). IEEE.
- Centobelli, P., Cerchione, R., Del Vecchio, P., Oropallo, E., & Secundo, G. (2022). Blockchain technology for bridging trust, traceability and transparency in circular supply chain. *Information & Management, 59*(7), 103508.
- Chen, X., & Lloyd, A. D. (2024). Understanding the challenges of Blockchain technology adoption: evidence from China's developing carbon markets. *Information Technology & People.*
- Ehmke, C., Wessling, F., & Friedrich, C. M. (2018, May). Proof-of-property: a lightweight and scalable Blockchain protocol. In *Proceedings of the 1st international workshop on emerging trends in software engineering for Blockchain* (pp. 48-51).
- Francisco, K., & Swanson, D. (2018). The supply chain has no clothes: Technology adoption of Blockchain for supply chain transparency. *Logistics, 2*(1), 2.
- Gschnaidtner, C., Dehghan, R., Hottenrott, H., & Schwierzy, J. (2024). Adoption and diffusion of Blockchain technology. *ZEW-Centre for European Economic Research Discussion Paper*, (24-018).
- Han, Y., & Fang, X. (2024). Systematic review of adopting Blockchain in supply chain management: bibliometric analysis and theme discussion. *International Journal of Production Research, 62*(3), 991-1016.
- Hofmann, F., Wurster, S., Ron, E., & Böhmecke-Schwafert, M. (2017, November). The immutability concept of Blockchains and benefits of early standardization. In *2017 ITU Kaleidoscope: Challenges for a Data-Driven Society (ITU K)* (pp. 1-8). IEEE.
- Ifeanyichukwu, E. E. (2024). Technological Implementation in the Service Sector: A Case Study. In *Artificial Intelligence for Smart Technology in the Hospitality and Tourism Industry* (pp. 305-336). Apple Academic Press.
- Jaradat, Z., Al-Hawamleh, A., Al Shbail, M. O., & Hamdan, A. (2024). Does the adoption of Blockchain technology add intangible benefits to the industrial sector? Evidence from Jordan. *Journal of Financial Reporting and Accounting, 22*(2), 327-349.

- Jimenez-Castillo, L., Sarkis, J., Saberi, S., & Yao, T. (2024). Blockchain-based governance implications for ecologically sustainable supply chain management. *Journal of Enterprise Information Management, 37*(1), 76-99.
- Joshi, A., Ranade, M., Patvardhan, N., & Sharma, P. (2024, February). An Enquiry into the Adoption and Effectiveness of Blockchain Technology in Trade Finance. In *2024 IEEE International Students' Conference on Electrical, Electronics and Computer Science (SCEECS)* (pp. 1-7). IEEE.
- Karadag, B., Zaim, A. H., & Akbulut, A. (2024). Blockchain in Finance: A Systematic Literature Review.
- Khajouei, H., Taghavifard, M. T., Amiri, M., & Raeesi Vanani, I. (2024). Identification of Stakeholders in Personal Health Records Using Blockchain Technology: A Comprehensive Review. *Journal of Information Technology Management, 16*(2), 181-205.
- Le, T. V., & Hsu, C. L. (2021). A systematic literature review of Blockchain technology: Security properties, applications and challenges. *Journal of Internet Technology, 22*(4), 789-802.
- Leng, J., Zhou, M., Zhao, J. L., Huang, Y., & Bian, Y. (2020). Blockchain security: A survey of techniques and research directions. *IEEE Transactions on Services Computing, 15*(4), 2490-2510.
- Li, X., Zhou, Y., & Yuen, K. F. (2024). Blockchain implementation in the maritime industry: critical success factors and strategy formulation. *Maritime Policy & Management, 51*(2), 304-322.
- Liu, X., Shah, R., Shandilya, A., Shah, M., & Pandya, A. (2024). A systematic study on integrating Blockchain in healthcare for electronic health record management and tacking medical supplies. *Journal of Cleaner Production*, 141371.
- Mukherjee, P., & Pradhan, C. (2021). Blockchain 1.0 to Blockchain 4.0—The evolutionary transformation of Blockchain technology. In *Blockchain technology: applications and challenges* (pp. 29-49). Cham: Springer International Publishing.
- Nakonechnyi, V., Toliupa, S., Saiko, V., Lutsenko, V., Ghno, G. S. N., & Hussain, A. K. (2024, April). Blockchain Implementation in the Protection System of Banking System During Online Banking Operations. In *2024 35th Conference of Open Innovations Association (FRUCT)* (pp. 492-500). IEEE.
- Politou, E., Casino, F., Alepis, E., & Patsakis, C. (2019). Blockchain mutability: Challenges and proposed solutions. *IEEE Transactions on Emerging Topics in Computing, 9*(4), 1972-1986.

- Qadri, S. M. (2024). CineCoin: Blockchain-Based Secure Digital Contents Distribution System.
- Rakhmonov, I. U., Kurbonov, N. N., & Elmuratov, T. A. (2024). Innovative Applications of Blockchain Technology in the Electrical Energy Sector. *Modern Science and Research, 3*(1), 1-5.
- Rijanto, A. (2024). Blockchain technology roles to overcome accounting, accountability and assurance barriers in supply chain finance. *Asian Review of Accounting*.
- Ryan, J. J., & Smith, S. S. (2021). History of Blockchain. In *The Emerald Handbook of Blockchain for Business* (pp. 15-29). Emerald Publishing Limited.
- Ryu, S. (2024). *Media and Entertainment Industry Management: How to Integrate Business and Management with Creativity and Imagination*. Taylor & Francis.
- Sayeed, S., & Marco-Gisbert, H. (2019). Assessing Blockchain consensus and security mechanisms against the 51% attack. *Applied sciences, 9*(9), 1788.
- Settipalli, L., Gangadharan, G. R., & Bellamkonda, S. (2024). An extended lightweight Blockchain based collaborative healthcare system for fraud prevention. *Cluster Computing, 27*(1), 563-573.
- Shah, P., Mishra, S., & Adrian, A. M. (2024). Utilization of Blockchain Technology in Artificial Intelligence–Based Healthcare Security. *Blockchain Transformations: Navigating the Decentralized Protocols Era*, 15-45.
- Shahzad, K., Zhang, Q., Ashfaq, M., Zafar, A. U., & Ahmad, B. (2024). Pre-to post-adoption of Blockchain technology in supply chain management: Influencing factors and the role of firm size. *Technological Forecasting and Social Change, 198*, 122989.
- Sharad Mangrulkar, R., & Vijay Chavan, P. (2024). Introduction to Blockchain. In *Blockchain Essentials: Core Concepts and Implementations* (pp. 1-46). Berkeley, CA: Apress.
- Sharma, B., Sekharan, C. N., & Zuo, F. (2018, November). Merkle-tree based approach for ensuring integrity of electronic medical records. In *2018 9th IEEE Annual Ubiquitous Computing, Electronics & Mobile Communication Conference (UEMCON)* (pp. 983-987). IEEE.
- Shinde, R., Patil, S., Kotecha, K., Potdar, V., Selvachandran, G., & Abraham, A. (2024). Securing AI-based healthcare systems using Blockchain technology: A state-of-the-art systematic literature review and future

research directions. *Transactions on Emerging Telecommunications Technologies*, *35*(1), e4884.

- Sibanda, B., Basheka, B., & van Romburgh, J. (2024). Enhancing governance through Blockchain technology in the South African public sector. *Africa's Public Service Delivery & Performance Review*, *12*(1), 10.
- Singh, K., Krishna, C., & Kumar, D. (2024). Professional Ethics, Challenges and Opportunities for Blockchain Technology in Healthcare Sector: A Systematic Review. *Recent Advances in Computer Science and Communications (Formerly: Recent Patents on Computer Science)*, *17*(1), 72-86.
- Siriphen, S., Chandarasupsang, T., Tananchana, A., Ramasamy, S. S., & Dawod, A. Y. (2024). Social Media Sentiments of Real Estate Investment on Blockchain Technology in Post-COVID-19. *International Journal of Intelligent Systems and Applications in Engineering*, *12*(5s), 347-359.
- Stamatakis, D., Kogias, D. G., Papadopoulos, P., Karkazis, P. A., & Leligou, H. C. (2024). Blockchain-Powered Gaming: Bridging Entertainment with Serious Game Objectives. *Computers*, *13*(1), 14.
- Syed, A. M. (2024). Distribution of PropTech Benefits to Stakeholders of Real Estate Market. In *Blockchain in Real Estate: Theoretical Advances and New Empirical Applications* (pp. 169-178). Singapore: Springer Nature Singapore.
- Trequattrini, R., Palmaccio, M., Turco, M., & Manzari, A. (2024). The contribution of Blockchain technologies to anti-corruption practices: A systematic literature review. *Business Strategy and the Environment*, *33*(1), 4-18.
- Tripathi, G., Ahad, M. A., & Casalino, G. (2023). A comprehensive review of Blockchain technology: underlying principles and historical background with future challenges. *Decision Analytics Journal*, 100344.
- Tüzün, O., & Ekinci, R. (2024). Blockchain Applications in Finance. In *Exploring Blockchain Applications* (pp. 162-183). CRC Press.
- Tyagi, A. K., Kukreja, S., Richa, & Sivakumar, P. (2024). Role of Blockchain Technology in Smart Era: A Review on Possible Smart Applications. *Journal of Information & Knowledge Management*, 2450032.
- Ulya, I. N., Hidayah, E. R. A., & Sari, R. I. (2024). Industrial Revolution Technology 4.0: The Concept Of Blockchain Accounting To Detect Corruption In Government Public Sector Finance. *International Journal Of Accounting, Management, And Economics Research*, *2*(1), 81-92.

- Vazquez Melendez, E. I., Bergey, P., & Smith, B. (2024). Blockchain technology for supply chain provenance: increasing supply chain efficiency and consumer trust. *Supply Chain Management: An International Journal.*
- Viriyasitavat, W., & Hoonsopon, D. (2019). Blockchain characteristics and consensus in modern business processes. *Journal of Industrial Information Integration, 13,* 32-39.
- Wamba, S. F., Wamba-Taguimdje, S. L., Lu, Q., & Queiroz, M. M. (2024). How emerging technologies can solve critical issues in organizational operations: An analysis of Blockchain-driven projects in the public sector. *Government Information Quarterly, 41*(1), 101912.
- Wang, W., Hoang, D. T., Hu, P., Xiong, Z., Niyato, D., Wang, P., ... & Kim, D. I. (2019). A survey on consensus mechanisms and mining strategy management in Blockchain networks. *Ieee Access, 7,* 22328-22370.
- Xie, J., Tang, H., Huang, T., Yu, F. R., Xie, R., Liu, J., & Liu, Y. (2019). A survey of Blockchain technology applied to smart cities: Research issues and challenges. *IEEE communications surveys & tutorials, 21*(3), 2794-2830.
- Yeow, K., Gani, A., Ahmad, R. W., Rodrigues, J. J., & Ko, K. (2017). Decentralized consensus for edge-centric internet of things: A review, taxonomy, and research issues. *IEEE Access, 6,* 1513-1524.
- YU, H. (2024). Integrating Blockchain Technology with Project Management System in the AEC Sector.
- Zarrin, J., Wen Phang, H., Babu Saheer, L., & Zarrin, B. (2021). Blockchain for decentralization of internet: prospects, trends, and challenges. *Cluster Computing, 24*(4), 2841-2866.
- Zhang, L., Ci, L., Wu, Y., & Wiwatanapataphee, B. (2024). The real estate time-stamping and registration system based on ethereum Blockchain. *Blockchain: Research and Applications, 5*(1), 100175.

Blockchain as an enabling technology

LEARNING OBJECTIVES

- Explain the differences between public, private, and consortium Blockchains
- Compare the scalability and security of different types of Blockchain technologies
- Evaluate the suitability of different Blockchain types for various use cases

3.0 Introduction

Blockchain technology, originally conceptualized as the underlying structure for cryptocurrencies like Bitcoin, has evolved into a transformative force across various industries. Its unique attributes—decentralization, transparency, immutability, and security—position Blockchain as a pivotal enabling technology capable of driving significant innovation and efficiency improvements.

3.1 Definitions of Blockchain as an enabling technology

Blockchain is a distributed, decentralized, and tamper-proof digital ledger that enables secure, transparent, and peer-to-peer transactions between participants.

David Gerard

Blockchain is a shared, immutable ledger that facilitates the process of recording transactions and tracking assets in a business network. It acts as a decentralized platform, enabling secure, transparent, and efficient collaboration between multiple parties.

Don Tapscott and Alex Tapscott

Blockchain serves as a distributed database or digital ledger that maintains an ever-growing list of data records. It enables secure, tamper-proof, and transparent data sharing and transactions, making it ideal for various applications, including cryptocurrencies and supply chain management.

Bettina Warburg

Blockchain is a distributed ledger technology that allows multiple participants to jointly manage a verifiable, append-only data ledger, enabling trust, security, and transparency in diverse sectors, including financing, supply chains, and administration.

William Mougayar

3.2 Significance of enabling Blockchain technology:

Blockchain technology is a ground-breaking innovation with far-reaching implications across various industries. Here's why Blockchain is considered such a significant enabling technology:

1. Decentralization: Traditional systems rely on centralized authorities to validate transactions and maintain records. Blockchain, however, distributes this responsibility across a network of nodes, eliminating the need for intermediaries. This decentralization enhances security, transparency, and trust in transactions.

2. Immutability: Once data is stored on a Blockchain, it is immutable and cannot be modified or removed. The immutability of the Blockchain guarantees the authenticity and reliability of the stored information, making it highly resistant to fraud and tampering.

3.Transparency: Every transaction on a Blockchain is visible to all participants in the network. This transparency fosters accountability and reduces the potential for corruption, as it becomes easier to trace the origin and movement of assets.

4. Security: Blockchain employs cryptographic techniques to secure transactions and data. Each block is linked to the previous one through cryptographic hashes, creating a chain of blocks that is extremely resistant to hacking and unauthorized access.

5. Cost Efficiency: By eliminating intermediaries and automating processes through smart contracts, Blockchain technology can significantly reduce transaction costs. This is particularly beneficial in industries like finance, supply chain management, and healthcare, where intermediaries add layers of complexity and expense.

6. Traceability and Audibility: Blockchain facilitates the monitoring and tracing of assets from their inception to their final stage, from production to consumption. In the management of the supply chain, where it may be used to detect inefficiencies, lessen counterfeiting, and guarantee regulatory compliance, traceability is extremely beneficial.

7. Inclusive Financial Services: Blockchain technology has the capacity to expand financial services to populations worldwide who do not have access to traditional banking or have limited access to banking services. Through Blockchain-based solutions like cryptocurrencies and decentralized finance (DeFi), individuals without access to traditional banking systems can participate in global financial transactions and access a range of financial services.

8. Smart Contracts: Smart contracts are self-executing contracts with the terms of the agreement directly written into code. These contracts automatically enforce and execute the terms of an agreement when predefined conditions are met, eliminating the need for intermediaries and streamlining processes across various industries.

9. Interoperability: Blockchain technology is evolving to become more interoperable, allowing different Blockchain networks to communicate and interact with each other seamlessly. This interoperability opens up new possibilities for collaboration and innovation across diverse sectors.

3.3 Types of Enabling Blockchain Technology

Blockchain technology has evolved beyond its initial roots in cryptocurrency, and today, we see numerous types of Blockchains enabling a wide range of applications. Each type of Blockchain has unique characteristics and is designed to address specific needs and use cases. Here, we explore some of the most prominent types of Blockchains, highlighting their distinct features and use cases.

3.3.1 Public Blockchain

A public Blockchain is a type of decentralized ledger technology that serves as an enabling platform for a wide range of applications and use cases. As an enabling technology, the public Blockchain brings forth several key features and characteristics that empower users and developers, creating a foundation for innovative solutions.

Examples: Bitcoin, Ethereum.

Definition: A distributed, public, and decentralized ledger is known as a public Blockchain. It allows anyone to participate in the network, validate transactions, and access the data stored on the ledger.

Key Features:

Decentralization and Transparency: Public Blockchains are authentically decentralized, signifying that the network is not under the control of any singular entity otherwise central authority. Transparency and immutability are guaranteed since each member of the network has access to the same data and is able to check transactions.

The technology's distributed architecture eliminates the necessity for intermediaries, thereby enabling users to retain control over their data, resources, and activities.

Open and Permission less Participation: Anyone with an Internet connection can join and participate in a public Blockchain network without seeking permission. This openness fosters inclusivity and enables global participation. Users from different regions can interact and transact directly with each other without geographical restrictions.

Smart Contract Functionality: Smart contracts, which are self-executing contracts that autonomously enforce agreed-upon terms and conditions, is supported by numerous public Blockchains, including Ethereum. Smart contracts enable a wide range of decentralized applications (dApps) to be built on top of the Blockchain. These dApps can revolutionize industries by automating processes, reducing intermediaries, and increasing trust and efficiency.

Trust and Security: Public Blockchains employ cryptographic algorithms and consensus mechanisms to ensure the security and integrity of the network. The network's dispersed nature ensures a high level of resilience against assaults or breakdowns, as it lacks a single point of failure. The transparency of the ledger allows for easy verification of transactions, enhancing trust among participants.

Censorship Resistance and Freedom: Due to their decentralized nature, public Blockchains provide censorship resistance. Freedom of expression and protection against censorship are guaranteed by the inability of any person or organization to change or censor transactions or data saved on the Blockchain.

Community and Collaboration: Public Blockchains often have vibrant and active communities of developers, enthusiasts, and users. This community aspect fosters collaboration, innovation, and the sharing of ideas. Additionally, It contributes to the growth and progression of the Blockchain ecosystem, fostering a network effect that positively impacts all participants.

Foundation for Web3 and Decentralized Finance (DeFi): Public Blockchains serve as the foundation for the emerging Web3 and DeFi movements. They enable users to own their digital assets, earn yields, access decentralized lending and borrowing platforms, and participate in decentralized governance, all without relying on traditional financial intermediaries.

A public Blockchain is an enabling technology that empowers users by providing decentralization, transparency, security, and trust. It opens up new opportunities for innovation, collaboration, and the creation of decentralized applications and solutions across various industries.

3.3.2 Private Blockchain

A private Blockchain is a type of Blockchain technology that differs from public Blockchains like Bitcoin or Ethereum in terms of its accessibility, permission structure, and governance mechanisms. It is characterized by its private and restricted nature, where access is limited to authorized participants. Here's how private Blockchains enable technology and its potential use cases.

Definition: A private Blockchain is a permissioned ledger controlled by a single organization or a central authority. Network and information access is limited, and modifications to the ledger are subject to the authority's approval.

Key Features:

A private Blockchain is a type of Blockchain technology that differs from public Blockchains like Bitcoin or Ethereum in terms of its accessibility, permission structure, and governance mechanisms. Here's how private Blockchains enable technology and use cases:

1. ***Controlled Accessibility:*** Private Blockchains restrict access to authorized participants only. Unlike public Blockchains, where anyone can join and participate, private Blockchains are often utilized by specific organizations, groups of companies, or consortiums. This controlled access ensures privacy and allows participants to share data and conduct transactions in a more controlled and secure environment.

2. ***Enhanced Privacy and Confidentiality:*** Due to their restricted access, private Blockchains offer enhanced privacy for transactions and data storage. Only authorized nodes can view and validate transactions, which can be particularly important for businesses dealing with sensitive information. Smart contracts in private Blockchains can also enforce confidentiality, ensuring that only relevant parties can access certain data.

3. ***Improved Performance:*** Private Blockchains often exhibit better performance compared to public Blockchains. Since the number of nodes is limited, consensus mechanisms can be faster and more efficient. This makes private Blockchains suitable for applications that require high transaction throughput and low latency, such as enterprise-level supply chain management or financial transactions.

4. ***Customizability and Flexibility:*** Private Blockchains offer a high degree of customizability. The organizing entity can set specific rules, smart contract standards, and governance mechanisms to suit their use case. This flexibility allows private Blockchains to be tailored to meet the exact needs of the participating organizations.

5. ***Consortium and Collaboration:*** Private Blockchains enable collaboration between trusted parties. For example, a group of banks can form a consortium and create a private Blockchain for inter-bank transactions, reducing settlement times and improving security. Private Blockchains can also facilitate supply chain transparency and efficiency, with authorized participants tracking goods along the supply chain.

6. ***Regulatory Compliance:*** Private Blockchains can be designed to meet specific regulatory requirements. In industries with strict data privacy and compliance standards, such as healthcare or finance, private Blockchains enable secure data sharing while adhering to regulatory frameworks.

Private Blockchains enable technology by providing a secure, flexible, and controlled environment for authorized participants to transact and share data. They strike a balance between the decentralization of public Blockchains and the privacy and performance needs of enterprises and specific use cases.

3.3.3 Consortium Blockchain

A consortium Blockchain is a type of Blockchain architecture where the validation rights and control over the network are shared among a pre-selected group of nodes or participants, known as a consortium. This design addresses the limitations of public and private Blockchain networks by offering a more centralized yet collaborative approach

Examples: Used in banking consortia for cross-border payments, trade finance, and identity management.

Definition: A consortium Blockchain is a partially decentralized ledger managed by a group of organizations or entities, often referred to as a consortium. It combines aspects of both public and private Blockchains.

Key Features:

A consortium Blockchain is a type of Blockchain architecture where the validation rights and control over the network are shared among a group of pre-selected nodes or participants, forming a consortium. This distributed ledger technology is particularly well-suited for certain use cases due to its unique characteristics, and it can be considered an enabling technology for various industries.

Partial Decentralization: Consortium Blockchains offer a balance between the complete decentralization of public Blockchains and the centralized control of private Blockchains. By involving a group of trusted organizations or entities, it distributes power and decision-making, preventing any single entity from having total control. This partial decentralization maintains a level of trust and transparency while allowing for more efficient consensus and governance mechanisms.

Improved Privacy and Confidentiality: In a consortium Blockchain, the participating nodes are known and authorized, which allows for better privacy and confidentiality controls. Since the network is not open to the public, it becomes easier to manage and secure sensitive data. This feature is particularly attractive to businesses that want to leverage Blockchain technology for specific use cases but need to maintain data privacy and compliance with regulations.

Enhanced Collaboration and Trust: Consortium Blockchains enable collaboration between competing firms or organizations with common interests. They offer a secure and reliable setting for exchanging data and conducting transactions without the requirement of central mediators. This technology fosters trust and transparency among the consortium members, improving overall efficiency and reducing friction in business processes.

Scalability and Performance: Compared to public Blockchains, consortium Blockchains can offer improved scalability and performance. Since the number of nodes is limited and pre-defined, the consensus process can be faster and more efficient. This makes consortium Blockchains suitable for use cases that require higher transaction throughput and lower latency.

Regulation and Compliance: Consortium Blockchains can facilitate regulatory compliance and governance. With a controlled group of participants, it becomes easier to enforce industry-specific regulations, data privacy standards, and other compliance requirements. This feature is especially beneficial for industries with stringent regulatory frameworks, such as healthcare, finance, and supply chain management.

Customizability: Consortium Blockchains have the flexibility for customization to accommodate the distinct requirements of the organizations involved. This adaptability allows for the adjustment of rules, consensus mechanisms, and smart contracts to match the consortium's goals, thereby ensuring that the technology supports their particular use cases and business needs.

A consortium Blockchain functions as a facilitative tool, offering a secure, transparent, and cooperative platform for organizations to enhance and modernize their operations. It maintains equilibrium between decentralization and governance, thereby enhancing privacy, scalability, and adherence to regulations. These attributes render consortium Blockchains suitable for various enterprise and industry-oriented uses.

3.3.4 Hybrid Blockchain

A hybrid Blockchain combines elements of both public and private Blockchains. It offers the benefits of decentralization and transparency of public Blockchains, along with the control and privacy features of private Blockchains.

Examples: Used in healthcare for secure data sharing, supply chain management for tracking goods across different stakeholders, and digital identity solutions.

Definition:

A hybrid Blockchain combines elements of both public and private Blockchains, allowing for flexible control over data privacy and accessibility.

Key Features:

A hybrid Blockchain, as the name suggests, is a blend of permissioned and permission less Blockchain features designed to leverage the benefits of both types of Blockchains and mitigate their individual limitations. This type of Blockchain structure can be considered an enabling technology due to its flexibility, security, and ability to cater to a wide range of use cases.

Flexibility and Customization: Hybrid Blockchains provide a significant level of adaptability, allowing for customization to suit the specific needs of an organization or community. This customisation encompasses various features, including consensus procedures, smart contract capabilities, and participation models. This flexibility enables hybrid Blockchains to adapt to different regulatory and compliance requirements, making them attractive to enterprises and governments.

Privacy and Confidentiality: One of the primary benefits of hybrid Blockchains lies in their capacity to offer heightened privacy and confidentiality. While public Blockchains offer transparency, there are use cases that require sensitive data to be kept private. Hybrid Blockchains allow participants to control data visibility, ensuring that confidential information is shared only with relevant parties. This feature enables secure data sharing and verification without sacrificing privacy.

Efficient Collaboration: Hybrid Blockchains facilitate efficient collaboration between different organizations or stakeholders. They offer a secure and reliable setting for participants to share data, execute smart contracts, and automate processes. By leveraging Blockchain technology, hybrid platforms can improve interoperability and streamline workflows, reducing friction and enhancing overall efficiency.

Regulatory Compliance: Enabling regulatory compliance is a key feature of hybrid Blockchains. Unlike public Blockchains, which operate outside regulatory frameworks, hybrid Blockchains can be designed to comply with specific industry or geographic regulations. This is particularly important for industries with stringent data privacy and security requirements, such as healthcare, finance, and government sectors.

Scalability and Performance: Hybrid Blockchains aim to address the scalability challenges faced by public Blockchains. Through consensus mechanism optimizations and permissioned participation, hybrid Blockchains can achieve higher transaction throughput and faster confirmation times. This enables them to support enterprise-level applications and a larger number of users without sacrificing performance.

Community Engagement and Incentivization: Hybrid Blockchains can utilize tokenized incentive structures to engage and motivate participants. Through the distribution of tokens, stakeholders can be incentivized to contribute resources, data, or services to the network. This promotes community engagement and fosters a sustainable ecosystem.

Hybrid Blockchains serve as enabling technology by providing a flexible, secure, and customizable platform that addresses the diverse needs of organizations and communities. They facilitate collaboration, improve data security and privacy, and enable regulatory compliance. The ability to customize consensus mechanisms and participation models makes hybrid Blockchains adaptable to a wide range of use cases, empowering businesses and individuals to leverage Blockchain technology effectively.

3.3.5 Smart Contract Blockchain

Smart contracts are self-executing contracts with the terms of the agreement directly written into code. They run on Blockchain platforms, enabling automatic execution of transactions when predefined conditions are met, without the need for intermediaries. The decentralized, unchangeable ledger provided by Blockchain technology, the basis of cryptocurrencies like Bitcoin and Ethereum, guarantees the safe recording of transactions. Smart contracts leverage this infrastructure to bring automation and trust to various domains beyond finance, including supply chain management, healthcare, real estate, and more

Examples: Ethereum's introduction of smart contracts revolutionized "decentralized finance (DeFi)" and "non-fungible tokens (NFTs)".

Definition:

Smart contract Blockchains focus on enabling self-executing contracts, which are programs that automatically enforce agreements and transactions.

Key Features:

A smart contract is a self-executing contract that utilizes Blockchain technology to facilitate the secure, transparent, and efficient execution of agreements between two or more parties. It is considered an enabling technology as it has the potential to revolutionize traditional contract management and automate a wide range of processes, reducing the need for intermediaries and enhancing trust and security in various industries.

Automation and Efficiency: Smart contracts are digital programs that automatically execute predetermined actions when specific conditions are met. They eliminate the need for manual intervention and reduce the time and effort required to manage and enforce contracts. This automation enhances efficiency, streamlines processes, and reduces administrative costs.

Trust and Security: Blockchain technology, which underpins smart contracts, provides enhanced security and trust. Smart contracts are saved and duplicated over a decentralised network of nodes, ensuring their integrity and safety from unauthorised alterations. The distributed nature of Blockchain makes it nearly impossible to alter or manipulate contract terms without the consensus of all network participants. This feature ensures trust and reduces the risk of fraud and interference.

Transparency and Immutability: Smart contracts are transparent and immutable by design. Once a smart contract is deployed to the Blockchain, its code and terms become accessible to all members of the network. Any variations or transactions executed by the smart contract are permanently recorded and cannot be altered retroactively. This transparency enhances accountability, reduces disputes, and allows for easy audit trails.

Intermediary Disruption: Smart contracts possess the capability to cause significant upheaval in industries that heavily depend on intermediaries, like lawyers, notaries, and brokers. By automating contract execution and enforcement, smart contracts can reduce the need for third-party involvement. This disintermediation can lower transaction costs, increase speed, and minimize the potential for human error or bias.

Consistency and Accuracy: Smart contracts ensure that agreements are executed consistently and accurately every time. They eliminate interpretation errors and discrepancies that may arise from traditional contract language. The code-based nature of smart contracts provides clarity and precision, reducing the likelihood of contractual disputes.

Enhanced Functionality: Smart contracts can be integrated with other technologies, such as IoT devices, oracles, and digital wallets, to create more complex and innovative solutions. This makes it possible to develop decentralized apps, or dApps, and makes it easier to transmit information and value in a safe and reliable manner.

Intelligent contract By offering a safe, open, and effective method of managing contracts and transactions, Blockchain technology empowers and enables individuals. Its automated and distributed nature has the potential to revolutionize various industries, disrupt intermediaries, and create new opportunities for decentralized applications and business models.

Each type of Blockchain serves distinct purposes, and their enabling technologies provide the foundation for a diverse range of applications, shaping the future of decentralized systems and empowering individuals and organizations alike.

References

- Alshahrani, R., Shabaz, M., Khan, M. A., & Kadry, S. (2024). Enabling intrinsic intelligence, ubiquitous learning and Blockchain empowerment for trust and reliability in 6G network evolution. *Journal of King Saud University-Computer and Information Sciences, 36*(4), 102041.
- Alshahrani, S. M. (2024). Disrupting the Status Quo: Blockchain's Potential for Overhauling Conventional Academic Systems. *Arabian Journal for Science and Engineering*, 1-21.
- Anthony Jnr, B. (2024). Enhancing Blockchain interoperability and intraoperability capabilities in collaborative enterprise-a standardized

architecture perspective. *Enterprise Information Systems, 18*(3), 2296647.

- Bennet, D., Maria, L., Sanjaya, Y. P. A., & Zahra, A. R. A. (2024). Blockchain technology: Revolutionizing transactions in the digital age. *ADI Journal on Recent Innovation, 5*(2), 192-199.
- Biswas, K., Chowdhury, M. J. M., & Usman, M. (2024). Blockchain of Things: Benefits, Challenges and Future Directions. *Sensors, 24*(3), 934.
- Chithaluru, P., Al-Turjman, F., Dugyala, R., Stephan, T., Kumar, M., & Dhatterwal, J. S. (2024). An enhanced consortium Blockchain diversity mining technique for IoT metadata aggregation. *Future Generation Computer Systems, 152*, 239-253.
- Chu, X., Wang, R., Ren, L., Li, Y., & Zhang, S. (2024). Enabling joint distribution with Blockchain technology in last-mile logistics. *Computers & Industrial Engineering, 187*, 109832.
- Dhar Dwivedi, A., Singh, R., Kaushik, K., Rao Mukkamala, R., & Alnumay, W. S. (2024). Blockchain and artificial intelligence for 5G-enabled Internet of Things: Challenges, opportunities, and solutions. *Transactions on Emerging Telecommunications Technologies, 35*(4), e4329.
- Gawusu, S., Tando, M. S., Ahmed, A., Jamatutu, S. A., Mensah, R. A., Das, O., ... & Ackah, I. (2024). Decentralized energy systems and Blockchain technology: Implications for alleviating energy poverty. *Sustainable Energy Technologies and Assessments, 65*, 103795.
- Grobe, N., Moller, F., Schoormann, T., & Henke, M. (2024). Designing trust-enabling Blockchain systems for the inter-organizational exchange of capacity. *Decision Support Systems, 179*, 114182.
- Gulia, P., Gill, N. S., Yahya, M., Gupta, P., Shukla, P. K., & Shukla, P. K. (2024). Exploring the Potential of Blockchain Technology in an IoT-Enabled Environment: A Review. *IEEE Access, 12*, 31197-31227.
- Kanaparthi, V. (2024). Exploring the Impact of Blockchain, AI, and ML on Financial Accounting Efficiency and Transformation. *arXiv preprint arXiv:2401.15715.*
- Khan, A. A., Laghari, A. A., Baqasah, A. M., Alroobaea, R., Almadhor, A., Sampedro, G. A., & Kryvinska, N. (2024). Blockchain-enabled infrastructural security solution for serverless consortium fog and edge computing. *PeerJ Computer Science, 10*.
- Mlika, F., Karoui, W., & Romdhane, L. B. (2024). Blockchain solutions for trustworthy decentralization in social networks. *Computer Networks*, 110336.

- Oriekhoe, O. I., Ilugbusi, B. S., & Adisa, O. (2024). Ensuring global food safety: integrating Blockchain technology into food supply chains. *Engineering Science & Technology Journal*, *5*(3), 811-820.
- Ovezik, C., Karakostas, D., & Kiayias, A. (2024). SoK: A stratified approach to Blockchain decentralization. In *Financial Cryptography and Data Security 2024: Twenty-Eighth International Conference*. Springer.
- Pandey, A. K., Daultani, Y., & Pratap, S. (2024). Blockchain technology enabled critical success factors for supply chain resilience and sustainability. *Business Strategy and the Environment*, *33*(2), 1533-1554.
- Panghal, A., Pan, S., Vern, P., Mor, R. S., & Jagtap, S. (2024). Blockchain technology for enhancing sustainable food systems: a consumer perspective. *International Journal of Food Science & Technology*, *59*(5), 3461-3468.
- Safitri, K. (2024). BLOCKCHAIN TECHNOLOGY IN MARKETING: EXPLORING DECENTRALIZED SOLUTIONS FOR TRUST AND TRANSPARENCY: LITERATURE REVIEW STUDY. *INTERNATIONAL JOURNAL OF ECONOMIC LITERATURE*, *2*(3), 681-697.
- Singh, A. K., & Kumar, V. P. (2024). Analyzing the barriers for Blockchain-enabled BIM adoption in facility management using best-worst method approach. *Built Environment Project and Asset Management*, *14*(2), 164-183.
- Tyagi, A. K. (2024). Engineering Applications of Blockchain in This Smart Era. In *Enhancing Medical Imaging with Emerging Technologies* (pp. 180-196). IGI Global.
- Wang, M., Zhu, T., Zuo, X., Ye, D., Yu, S., & Zhou, W. (2024). Public and Private Blockchain Infusion: A Novel Approach to Federated Learning. *IEEE Internet of Things Journal*.
- Wang, X., Wu, Y. C., & Ma, Z. (2024). Blockchain in the courtroom: exploring its evidentiary significance and procedural implications in US judicial processes. *Frontiers in Blockchain*, *7*, 1306058.
- Xiao, N., Wang, Z., Sun, X., & Miao, J. (2024). A novel Blockchain-based digital forensics framework for preserving evidence and enabling investigation in industrial Internet of Things. *Alexandria Engineering Journal*, *86*, 631-643.

IV

Distributed Ledger Technologies in Blockchain

LEARNING OBJECTIVES

- Explain the concept of decentralization in distributed ledger technologies.
- How do distributed ledger technologies ensure data integrity and security?
- Describe the role of consensus mechanisms in maintaining the integrity of distributed ledgers

4.0 Introduction

Blockchain technology has revolutionized the way data and information are stored, shared, and secured, and at the heart of this revolution is Distributed Ledger Technology (DLT). DLT is a peer-to-peer system that synchronizes data across multiple nodes or sites, enabling transparent, secure, and tamper-proof data management. In the context of Blockchain, DLT serves as the foundational architecture, ensuring the integrity and authenticity of transactions and data.

4.1 Definitions

Distributed Ledger Technology (DLT) is a digital system for recording the transaction of assets in which the transactions and their details are recorded in multiple places at the same time. It differs from centralized ledger systems in that a centralized ledger is controlled by one entity and recorded in one place.

Moyano, 2017

Distributed Ledger Technologies (DLTs) are databases that independently record and track assets, transactions, or records across multiple nodes or sites, with no central coordinator or centralized data storage. Each node in the network has a copy of the ledger, and consensus protocols ensure that all copies are identical and secure.

Tapscott and Tapscott

A distributed ledger is a consensus of replicated, shared, and synchronized digital data spread across multiple sites, countries, or institutions. No one party owns or controls the data, and changes to the ledger are reflected identically across all nodes, making it virtually impossible to tamper with the data undetected.

Iansiti and Lakhani

4.2 Distributed Ledger Architectures

Distributed Ledgers are a type of database that is spread across multiple sites, regions, or participants. They allow for the secure and transparent recording of transactions and data across a decentralized network. Here are the main types of distributed ledger architectures:

1.Centralised Ledger

2. Decentralised Ledger

3. Distributed Ledger

1.Centralised Ledger

In a centralized ledger, all data is stored and managed by a single central authority. This model is common in traditional financial institutions.

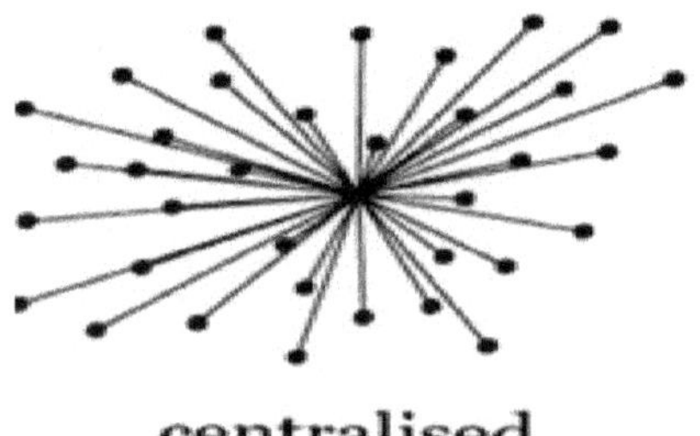

Source: Google; blockchain-council.org

2. Decentralised Ledger

In a decentralized ledger, each participant holds a copy of the ledger, but transactions must be validated by a central entity. This model is more secure than a centralized ledger because it reduces the risk of a single point of failure.

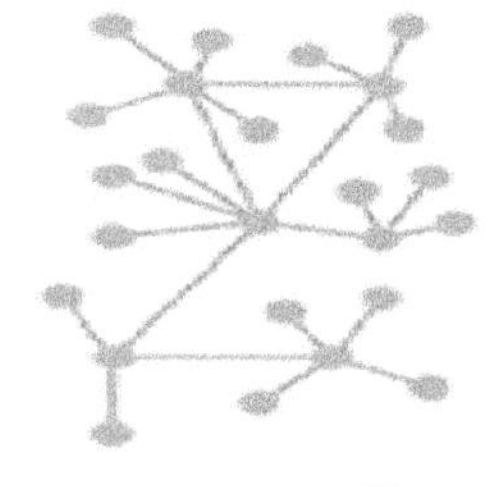

Source: Google; Quora

3. Distributed Ledger

In a distributed ledger, all participants have equal rights and hold a complete copy of the ledger. Each node independently validates transactions, and consensus mechanisms ensure agreement across the network. This model is the basis for blockchain technology.

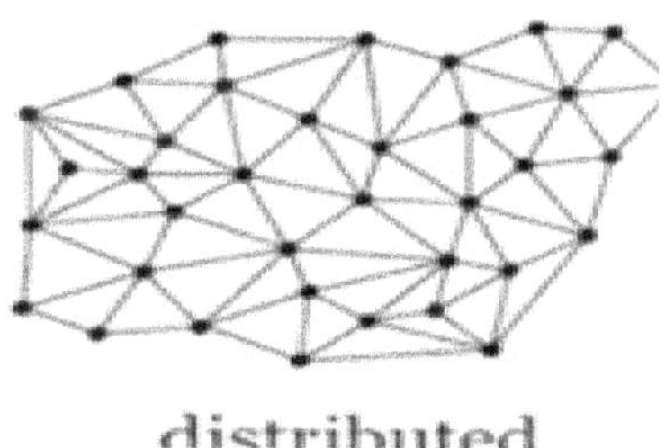

Source: Google; blockchain-council.org

4.3 Key Characteristics of DLT in Blockchain:

Decentralization: DLT does away with the requirement for a middleman or central authority. Rather, it disperses information throughout a network of interconnected nodes, each of which has a duplicate copy of the ledger. Because of this decentralization, the data is protected from being entirely controlled by one party, reducing the risk of data manipulation and enhancing transparency.

Consensus Mechanisms: One of the critical aspects of DLT is the use of consensus mechanisms. These mechanisms, such as evidence of work or Evidence of stake, provide consensus among all nodes regarding the legitimacy of transactions and the current status of the ledger. Through cryptographic algorithms and validation rules, consensus is reached, maintaining the integrity of the distributed ledger.

Immutable and Secure: DLT employs cryptographic hash functions to ensure data immutability. Once a transaction or data entry is recorded and validated, it is virtually impossible to modify or delete it without the alteration being visible to all nodes in the network. This immutability, combined with encryption techniques, enhances the security and auditability of the ledger.

Transparency and Auditability: DLT offers a clear and verifiable record of transactions or modifications to data. As all transactions are recorded on multiple nodes, it becomes difficult to conceal or manipulate data without detection. Enhanced transparency fosters trust and accountability, rendering it optimal for overseeing supply chains, conducting financial transactions, and maintaining records.

Smart Contracts and Automation: Blockchain distributed ledger technology (DLT) commonly integrates smart contracts, which are contracts that may execute themselves according to predetermined rules. These contracts employ automation to streamline numerous processes, hence decreasing the necessity for manual intervention and minimising errors. Smart contracts can be programmed to trigger actions based on specific conditions, ensuring trust and immutability in complex workflows.

4.4 Distributed Ledger Technologies Applications:

Applications of Distributed Ledger Technology (DLT)

Financial Transactions and Cryptocurrencies

Smart Contracts

Supply Chain Management

Digital Identity and Security

Voting and Governance

Inter-organizational Data Sharing

Tokenization and Asset Representation

DLT within Blockchain technology has been implemented across diverse sectors, such as finance, supply chain management, healthcare, and digital identity management. Its utilization facilitates secure and transparent transactions, enhances data exchange, and diminishes the need for intermediaries, thereby bolstering efficacy and fostering trust across numerous scenarios. Distributed Ledger Technology in Blockchain provides a robust framework for secure, transparent, and tamper-proof data management, revolutionizing the way information is exchanged and verified across industries. Distributed Ledger Technologies (DLT) are an essential element of the technology of Blockchain, and they have diverse uses in numerous industries. At its core, DLT refers to a decentralized system where data, information, or transactions are recorded and stored across multiple participants or "nodes" in a network. This distributed nature of DLT brings about several benefits and use cases, especially when coupled with Blockchain's secure and transparent characteristics. Some key applications of DLT in the context of Blockchain technology:

Financial Transactions and Cryptocurrencies: Blockchain's most well-known application is in the financial sector, particularly with cryptocurrencies like Bitcoin and Ethereum. Peer-to-peer secure transactions are made possible by DLT without the need for conventional middlemen like banks. Every transaction is meticulously documented on a distributed ledger, guaranteeing complete transparency, unchangeability, and protection against duplicitous actions.

Smart Contracts: Smart contracts are self-executing contracts that automatically enforce agreements between parties. DLT platforms, such as Ethereum, allow for the creation and deployment of smart contracts. These contracts can be coded to initiate actions according to predetermined criteria, so decreasing reliance on trusted intermediaries and minimising conflicts.

Supply Chain Management: Blockchain and DLT can enhance supply chain transparency, product traceability, and efficiency. By recording transactions and product movements on a distributed ledger, stakeholders can track goods along the supply chain, verify their authenticity, and ensure compliance with regulations. This application is especially beneficial in areas such as food safety, expensive products, and pharmaceutical.

Digital Identity and Security: Distributed Ledger Technology (DLT) offers a robust and decentralised framework for managing digital identities in a secure manner. Instead of depending on centralised databases that are susceptible to cyber attacks, DLT enables individuals to control and verify their personal information. This application has implications for secure authentication, KYC (Know Your Customer) processes, and secure data sharing.

Voting and Governance: Blockchain technology, utilizing DLT, can bring transparency and security to voting processes. DLT-based voting systems can prevent voter fraud, ensure vote immutability, and enhance voter privacy. Additionally, Blockchain can facilitate more efficient and transparent governance structures, enabling secure and verifiable decision-making processes.

Inter-organizational Data Sharing: DLT enables secure and trusted data sharing between organizations. This use is particularly valuable in areas such as medical care, where the secure sharing of patient data among several providers is necessary. DLT can also facilitate data monetization and data provenance in a secure and transparent manner.

Tokenization and Asset Representation: DLT enables the tokenization of assets, representing ownership and enabling their secure transfer. This application encompasses a broad spectrum of assets, including equities, real estate, and digital collectibles (NFTs). Tokenization can streamline asset trading, increase liquidity, and enhance transparency in ownership records.

These applications highlight the versatility and potential of DLT in Blockchain technology, showcasing how distributed ledger systems can revolutionize traditional processes across various sectors.

4.5 Advantages of Distributed Ledger Technologies (DLT)

Blockchain technology is one of the Distributed Ledger Technologies (DLT) features that help a wide range of businesses. These are a few of DLT's main benefits.

Advantages of Distributed Ledger Technology (DLT)

1. Decentralization and Transparency
2. Immutability and Security
3. Enhanced Traceability and Auditability
4. Smart Contracts and Automation
5. Consensus and Collaboration
6. Efficiency and Cost Reduction
7. Data Privacy and Ownership

Disadvantage of DLT

1. Computational Power and Energy Consumption
2. Transaction Speed and Scalability
3. Regulatory and Legal Challenges
4. Complexity and Technical Expertise
5. Interoperability and Standards

6. Data Privacy and Immutability
7. Governance and Consensus

Decentralization and Transparency: Distributed Ledger Technology (DLT), utilising Blockchain, guarantees the dispersion of data among numerous nodes or participants within a network. The absence of central authorities or middlemen is a result of the decentralised character. Every participant has access to the same real-time data, enhancing transparency and trust. This transparency can improve auditability and reduce fraud risks.

Immutability and Security: The immutability of data is a fundamental advantage of DLT. Once a transaction or data entry is verified and entered on the distributed ledger, it remains immutable and transparent to all network participants. The cryptographic security mechanisms inherent in Blockchain technology make it extremely secure and resilient to cyber-attacks and data breaches.

Enhanced Traceability and Auditability: DLT offers a comprehensive and clear audit trail of every single transaction or data change. This traceability improves supply chain management, logistics, and any industry requiring product tracking. It enables efficient tracking of assets, goods, or transactions, enhancing visibility and simplifying audit processes.

Smart Contracts and Automation: Smart contracts, which are autonomous agreements with predefined principles, are made possible by Blockchain-based DLT. Smart contracts automate a variety of processes, thereby minimising the need for manual interventions and the resulting errors. They can be used for digital identity management, supply chain contracts, financial agreements, and more, improving efficiency and reducing costs.

Consensus and Collaboration: Consensus mechanisms are employed by DLT networks to verify transactions and guarantee consensus among network participants. This consensus-driven approach fosters collaboration and trust between different entities, even if they do not fully trust each other. It enables multiple stakeholders to work together securely and efficiently, sharing data and processes with confidence.

Efficiency and Cost Reduction: Through the elimination of intermediaries and the optimisation of processes, Distributed Ledger Technology (DLT) has the capacity to greatly enhance efficiency and decrease operational expenses. This is particularly beneficial in industries with complex, multi-party transactions, like supply chain management, real estate, and financial management. DLT can also reduce administrative burdens and speed up settlement processes.

Data Privacy and Ownership: DLT empowers individuals to retain authority over their data and decide which details to disclose. This decentralized method of storing and handling data improves confidentiality and grants users autonomy over their digital assets and personal data across various applications.

These advantages make DLT and Blockchain technology attractive solutions for various use cases across industries, ranging from government to health care, banking, and supply chain management, among others.

4.6 Disadvantages of Distributed Ledger Technologies (DLT)

While Distributed Ledger Technologies (DLT) in Blockchain offer a range of potential benefits, there are also some disadvantages and challenges to consider:

Computational Power and Energy Consumption: One of the most widely discussed disadvantages of DLT, specifically in public Blockchains, is the substantial computational power and energy required for the consensus process, particularly in proof-of-work (PoW) systems. The process of mining or reaching consensus can consume a substantial amount of power, raising questions about these technologies' long-term viability and potential effects on the environment.

Transaction Speed and Scalability: DLTs, especially in their early implementations, often face challenges in terms of transaction speed and scalability. The process of reaching consensus across a distributed network can result in slower transaction processing times compared to traditional centralized systems, especially when the network experiences high volumes of transactions. This can limit the practicality of DLT for applications that require high throughput.

Regulatory and Legal Challenges: The decentralized nature of DLT can pose regulatory and legal challenges. The lack of a central authority makes it difficult for governments and regulatory bodies to oversee and control activities on Blockchain networks. Issues related to taxation, anti-money laundering, and know-your-customer (KYC) regulations need to be carefully addressed to ensure compliance without compromising the benefits of decentralization.

Complexity and Technical Expertise: Implementing and managing DLT solutions often require a high level of technical expertise. The complexity of setting up and maintaining a distributed ledger system can be a barrier for organisations, particularly small and medium-sized firms, that have insufficient resources and a shortage of competent individuals. This complexity may also hinder user adoption, as interacting with Blockchain-based systems might be less intuitive for users unfamiliar with the technology.

Interoperability and Standards: The lack of standardized protocols and interoperability between different Blockchain platforms and distributed ledger solutions can hinder the exchange of data and limit the potential for collaboration. This fragmentation can lead to siloed systems and limit the network effects that are crucial for the success of Blockchain ecosystems.

Data Privacy and Immutability: While Blockchain's immutability is often touted as a benefit, it can also present challenges when it comes to data privacy and the right to be forgotten. Once data is recorded on a distributed ledger, it becomes challenging, if not impossible, to modify or delete, even if there are valid reasons for doing so, such as complying with data privacy regulations or correcting erroneous information.

Governance and Consensus: Determining the rules and governance models for a distributed ledger system can be complex, especially in public Blockchains. Reaching consensus on protocol changes or upgrades can be challenging and may require a strong level of synchronisation and consensus among network participants.

References

- Akram, W., Joshi, R., Haider, T., Sharma, P., Jain, V., Garud, N., & Narwaria, N. S. (2024). Blockchain technology: A potential tool for the management of pharma supply chain. *Research in Social and Administrative Pharmacy.*
- Bacon, L., & Tarr, J. A. (2024). Distributed Ledger Technology and Blockchain: Insurance. *The Global Insurance Market and Change*, 95-126.
- Baninemeh, E., Jansen, S., & Labunets, K. (2024). A Security Risk Assessment Method for Distributed Ledger Technology (DLT) based Applications: Three Industry Case Studies. *arXiv preprint arXiv:2401.12358.*
- Bellaj, B., Ouaddah, A., Bertin, E., Crespi, N., & Mezrioui, A. (2024). Drawing the boundaries between Blockchain and Blockchain-like systems: A Comprehensive Survey on distributed Ledger Technologies. *Proceedings of the IEEE, 112*(3), 247-299.
- Bhurgri, S. S., Ali, N. I., Korejo, I. A., & Brohi, I. A. (2024). Enhancing Security and Confidentiality in Decentralized Payment System Based on

Blockchain Technology. *The Asian Bulletin of Big Data Management*, *4*(1), Science-4.

- BUNDI, D. G., MUTUA, S. M., & KARUME, S. M. (2024). Underlying Consensus Algorithms, Architectures and Data Structures in Distributed Ledger Technologies Applications.
- Cheng, Q., Gong, Y., Qin, Y., Ao, X., & Li, Z. (2024). Secure Digital Asset Transactions: Integrating Distributed Ledger Technology with Safe AI Mechanisms. *Academic Journal of Science and Technology*, *9*(3), 156-161.
- Geng, Q., Chuai, Z., & Jin, J. (2024). Cross-organizational data exchange based on consortium Blockchain with consistency guarantee. *The Journal of Supercomputing*, 1-38.
- Herbe, A., Estermann, Z., Holzwarth, V., & vom Brocke, J. (2024). How to effectively use distributed ledger technology in supply chain management?. *International Journal of Production Research*, *62*(7), 2522-2547.
- Jain, P., & Jain, R. Revolutionary Finance: Impact of Blockchain and Distributed Ledger Technology on the Financial Industry. In *Convergence of Blockchain and Internet of Things in Healthcare* (pp. 146-161). CRC Press.
- Lin, D. (2024). Exploring the economic logic of the application scenario of Blockchain technology—Analysis based on the perspective of information economics. *Information Systems and Economics*, *5*(3), 9-14.
- Lin, M. B., Pele, D. T., & Ren, R. (2024). Understanding Blockchain Technology. *Available at SSRN 4804484*.
- Liu, J., & Wu, J. (2024). A Comprehensive Survey on Blockchain Technology and Its Applications. *Highlights in Science, Engineering and Technology*, *85*, 128-138.
- Madir, J. (2024). Smart contracts. In *FinTech* (pp. 244-267). Edward Elgar Publishing.
- McGurk, B., & Reichenbach, S. (2024). The application of DLT in financial services: Benefits and use cases. In *Financial Services Law and Distributed Ledger Technology* (pp. 64-90). Edward Elgar Publishing.
- Mishra, N. K., Sahoo, S., Agarwal, S., Sharma, P. P., & Ilahi, F. (2024). Impact of institutional pressures and security on Blockchain technology adoption and organization performance: an empirical study. *The Journal of Technology Transfer*, 1-26.
- Mohan, V., Khezr, P., & Berg, C. (2024). Voting with time commitment for decentralized governance: Bond voting as a Sybil-resistant mechanism. *Management Science*.

- Nita, S. L., & Mihailescu, M. I. (2024). A Novel Authentication Scheme Based on Verifiable Credentials Using Digital Identity in the Context of Web 3.0. *Electronics, 13*(6), 1137.
- Odimarha, A. C., Ayodeji, S. A., & Abaku, E. A. (2024). The role of technology in supply chain risk management: Innovations and challenges in logistics. *Magna Scientia Advanced Research and Reviews, 10*(2), 138-145.
- Oke, A. E., Aliu, J., Ehiosun, L. U., Kineber, A. F., & Stephen, S. S. (2024). Adoption of distributed ledger technology for construction projects: a study of the challenges in a developing country. *Journal of Engineering, Design and Technology.*
- Olaniyi, O. O. (2024). Ballots and padlocks: Building digital trust and security in democracy through information governance strategies and Blockchain technologies. *Available at SSRN 4759942.*
- Ramos, S., & Ellul, J. (2024). Blockchain for Artificial Intelligence (AI): enhancing compliance with the EU AI Act through distributed ledger technology. A cybersecurity perspective. *International Cybersecurity Law Review, 5*(1), 1-20.
- Rasool, S., Iqbal, M., Shancang, L., Dagiuklas, A., & Ghosh, S. (2024). Security, Privacy and Trust of Distributed Ledgers Technology. IEEE.
- Rijanto, A. (2024). Blockchain technology roles to overcome accounting, accountability and assurance barriers in supply chain finance. *Asian Review of Accounting.*
- Salama, R., Cacciagrano, D., & Al-Turjman, F. (2024, April). Blockchain and Financial Services a Study of the Applications of Distributed Ledger Technology (DLT) in Financial Services. In *International Conference on Advanced Information Networking and Applications* (pp. 124-135). Cham: Springer Nature Switzerland.
- Singh, V. K., & Singh, K. (2024). IoT-Based Distributed Sensor Networks: A Comprehensive Survey. *Journal of IoT-based Distributed Sensor Networks, 1*(1), 30-35.
- Somma, A., De Benedictis, A., Esposito, C., & Mazzocca, N. (2024). The convergence of Digital Twins and Distributed Ledger Technologies: A systematic literature review and an architectural proposal. *Journal of Network and Computer Applications*, 103857.
- Somma, A., De Benedictis, A., Esposito, C., & Mazzocca, N. (2024). The convergence of Digital Twins and Distributed Ledger Technologies: A systematic literature review and an architectural proposal. *Journal of*

Network and Computer Applications, 103857.

- Sreenath, G., Sridhar, G. T., Sannabhadti, A. A., SJ, R. M., & Kounte, M. R. (2024, January). Blockchain Based Digital Identity Solution. In *2024 2nd International Conference on Intelligent Data Communication Technologies and Internet of Things (IDCIoT)* (pp. 387-391). IEEE.
- Tkachuk, R. V., Ilie, D., Robert, R., Kebande, V., & Tutschku, K. (2024). On the performance and scalability of consensus mechanisms in privacy-enabled decentralized renewable energy marketplace. *Annals of Telecommunications*, *79*(3), 271-288.
- www.blockchain-council.org
- www.quora.com

V

Mining, Forking, and Sales in Blockchain technology

LEARNING OBJECTIVES

- Explain the process of mining a new block in a blockchain network
- Describe the role of miners in verifying and validating transactions
- Analyze the impact of forking on the decentralization and security of a blockchain network
- Explain how blockchain technology can be used to facilitate sales transactions.

5.1 Introduction

Mining is a fundamental process in Blockchain technology, crucial for the operation and security of decentralized networks like Bitcoin and Ethereum. At its core, mining involves validating and adding new transactions to the Blockchain ledger through the solution of complex mathematical puzzles. This process ensures the integrity and security of the network while simultaneously creating new cryptocurrency units. Miners, who are participants in the Blockchain network, use their computational power to solve cryptographic puzzles that validate transactions. These puzzles require significant computational effort and energy, a process known as Proof-of-Work (PoW). Upon solving the puzzle, a miner adds a new block of transactions to the Blockchain. This block, once verified by other nodes in the network, is appended to the existing chain, maintaining a consistent and tamper-proof ledger. Mining serves several critical functions. It provides a decentralized mechanism for achieving consensus on the transaction history without needing a central authority. This decentralization ensures that no single entity can control or manipulate the network. Moreover, mining secures the Blockchain against attacks and fraud, such as double-spending, by making it computationally impractical to alter past transactions. Incentives perform a substantial role in the mining process. Miners are rewarded with newly minted cryptocurrency coins and transaction fees from the transactions included in their blocks. This reward system encourages participation and investment in the necessary computational resources, fostering a robust and secure network. Mining algorithms can vary. While PoW relies on computational power, Proof-of-Stake (PoS) requires participants to lock their tokens as collateral, reducing the energy consumption associated with mining.

5.1.1 Definitions of Mining in Blockchain:

Mining is the process of adding transaction records to Bitcoin's public ledger of past transactions...

Nakamoto, S.

Miners are responsible for securing the Blockchain and are incentivized to do so by rewards in the form of newly created bitcoins...

Narayanan

Blockchain mining is the process of digitally adding transaction records to the distributed ledger of existing transactions. It's called mining because it is similar in concept to gold or diamond mining in the physical world, where miners have to dig for precious minerals.

Yuan, X

These explanations underscore the essential function of mining in upholding the integrity, security, and decentralization of Blockchain networks. Mining establishes an incentive system that promotes truthful engagement and enhances the overall efficacy and trustworthiness of Blockchain technology.

5.1.2 Features of Mining in Blockchain Technology

Mining ensures the integrity and security of Blockchain networks. It provides a decentralized and trustless mechanism for reaching consensus on the state of transactions, eliminating the need for central authorities. Additionally, mining incentivizes participants to contribute their computational resources to maintain and secure the network.

Decentralized Consensus: Mining plays a vital role in achieving decentralized consensus in a Blockchain network. Miners use computational power to validate transactions, creating a trustless and distributed system.

Security and Integrity: Mining is responsible for guaranteeing the confidentiality and authenticity of the Blockchain ledger. Through cryptographic puzzles and hash functions, miners secure the network against malicious attacks and double-spending.

Transaction Verification: Miners verify and confirm pending transactions on the network. By solving complex mathematical puzzles, They generate clusters of transactions that are then appended to the Blockchain.

Incentive Mechanism: Mining introduces an incentive structure to encourage honest participation in the network. Workers receive Bitcoin tokens as a reward for successfully validating and securing transactions.

Proof-of-Work (PoW) and Proof-of-Stake (PoS): Mining algorithms vary, with PoW requiring computational power to solve puzzles, while PoS relies on stakeholders locking their tokens as a commitment.

5.1.3 How Does Mining Work?

Blockchain technology has revolutionized digital transactions and data storage with its secure, decentralized nature. A key component that enables the functioning of Blockchain networks is the process of mining. Mining is the mechanism through which new blocks are added to the Blockchain, facilitating transaction verification and maintaining the network's integrity. This article seeks to offer an in-depth exploration of the mechanics behind mining in Blockchain technology. Fundamentally, mining entails the resolution of intricate computational challenges to authenticate transactions and fortify the integrity of the Blockchain network. Miners are network nodes or participants who employ their processing power to create new blocks and verify transactions. The mining process can be summarized in the following steps:

Transaction Collection and Propagation: Miners collect new transactions broadcasted across the network and assemble them into a block. Each transaction contains information such as the sender's address, the recipient's address, and the amount to be transferred.

Hashing and Puzzle Solving: Once the transactions are grouped into a block, miners use a cryptographic hash function to generate a unique hash for the block. The hash function receives the information from the block and converts it into a hash code of a consistent length. To add a block to the Blockchain, miners must solve a complex mathematical puzzle by finding a hash that meets certain conditions (e.g., starting with a specific number of zeros).

Proof of Work (PoW) and Consensus: The process of solving the puzzle is often referred to as "Proof of Work." It requires significant computational power and energy, serving as a deterrent to malicious actors attempting to manipulate the network. Once a miner finds a valid solution (proof-of-work), they broadcast it to the entire network. Other nodes verify the solution and, if valid, add the new block to their copy of the Blockchain. This achieves consensus among the distributed nodes, ensuring everyone has the same transaction history.

Block Reward and Transaction Fees: As an incentive mechanism, miners who successfully add a block to the Blockchain are rewarded with cryptocurrency coins or tokens. This reward is known as the "block reward." Additionally, miners also receive transaction fees associated with the transactions included in the block.

Network Security and Decentralization: The security and decentralization of the Blockchain network are vitally dependent on mining. The computational puzzle-solving process makes it extremely difficult for any single entity to control a majority of the network's computing power. This distributed consensus mechanism ensures that any malicious activity or data tampering would require an impractical amount of computational power to override the network's consensus.

Mining serves as the fundamental support for Blockchain technology, guaranteeing the reliability, security, and decentralisation of the network. Through the process of solving complex puzzles and reaching a consensus, miners secure the transaction history and are incentivized for their contributions. Blockchain technology is constantly advancing, and mining plays a crucial role in driving the wider use of cryptocurrencies and decentralised apps.

5.1.4 Process of Mining in Blockchain Technology

Blockchain technology relies on a process known as mining to secure and grow its distributed digital ledger system. Mining is a crucial component that enables Blockchain to function as a decentralized and secure system. Here is a simplified explanation of the process of mining in Blockchain technology:

1. Introduction to Mining: Blockchain mining is a computational process by which transactions are verified and added to a Blockchain network's digital ledger. Miners are individuals or groups who use their computing power to validate and secure the Blockchain.

2. Transaction Broadcasting: When a transaction begins on a Blockchain network, it is disseminated to all terminals or participants in the network. For example, if someone sends cryptocurrency to another person, this transaction information is transmitted across the network.

3. Transaction Verification: Miners receive these broadcasted transactions and start the verification process. They check if the transaction is valid, confirming that the sender has the necessary funds and has not already spent those funds in another transaction. Miners also verify that the transaction conforms to the network's rules and does not contain any malicious or incorrect data.

4. Competing to Solve Cryptographic Puzzles: After verifying transactions, miners compete to add blocks of transactions to the Blockchain ledger. This involves solving complex cryptographic puzzles through computational power. Miners use their hardware to guess a unique code called a hash that, when combined with the transaction data, produces an acceptable hash value. Finding this hash requires significant computational resources and is often likened to guessing a complex password.

5. Consensus Mechanisms: The first miner or mining pool that solves the puzzle and finds a valid hash announces it to the network. Other nodes then verify the solution independently. If the majority of nodes agree that the solution is correct and the transactions are valid, consensus is achieved, and the block is added to the Blockchain. This process ensures that everyone's copy of the ledger remains identical.

6. Block Reward and Transaction Fees: The successful miner or mining pool that adds a block receives a reward in the form of newly minted cryptocurrency units (e.g., bitcoins) and transaction fees attached to the transactions included in the block. This incentivizes miners to participate in the mining process and support the network.

7. Increasing Blockchain Security: As more blocks are incorporated into the network, the security of the Blockchain escalates. This is due to the increasing complexity of computational challenges, which in turn hinders the capacity of malicious actors to alter transaction data. This also ensures that miners continue to invest in more powerful hardware to keep up with the network's demands.

8. Decentralized Nature: Anyone who possesses the requisite hardware is permitted to engage in mining and an internet connection, contributing to the decentralized nature of Blockchain technology. This distributed mining process makes Blockchain networks more resilient and less susceptible to centralized control or attacks.

Blockchain mining is a process that combines cryptography, computational power, and consensus mechanisms to secure and expand a Blockchain network while incentivizing participants through rewards. This innovative process forms the backbone of Blockchain technology, enabling trust, security, and decentralization in various applications.

Forking

5.2 Introduction

In the context of blockchain technology, forking refers to the process of creating a new version of the blockchain protocol, resulting in a divergence from the existing blockchain. This divergence occurs when a group of developers or stakeholders make changes to the protocol's rules, leading to a split in the blockchain's transaction history.

There are two main types of forks:

1.Soft Fork: In a soft fork, the changes made to the protocol are backward-compatible, meaning that nodes running the updated software can still interact with nodes running the older version. Soft forks typically result in a temporary divergence of the blockchain, but eventually, consensus is reached, and the shorter chain is abandoned. Soft forks usually aim to tighten rules or add new features without disrupting the existing network.

2. **Hard Fork**: In a hard fork, the changes made to the protocol are not backward-compatible, meaning that nodes running the updated software cannot interact with nodes running the older version and vice versa. This results in a permanent split in the blockchain, creating two separate networks with different transaction histories. Hard forks are often used to introduce significant changes to the protocol, such as altering the consensus mechanism, increasing block size, or reversing transactions.

5.2.1 Definitions

A fork is a change in a computer program's protocol affecting how that program validates data and, in the case of cryptocurrency, how nodes on a distributed network reach consensus regarding transaction validity.

Paul McFedries

Blockchain forking refers to a divergence in the Blockchain network that occurs when two or more blocks have the same hash value, creating multiple potential paths for the Blockchain to follow.

William Mougayar

These definitions highlight the key aspects of forking in Blockchain technology, including its relationship to protocol changes, network consensus, and the potential creation of alternative chains or cryptocurrencies.

5.2.2 The significance of forking in Blockchain technology

The concept of "forking" is an essential mechanism in Blockchain technology, and it holds significant value in the world of decentralized systems and cryptocurrencies. Forking can be defined as a process where a Blockchain network undergoes a rule change, resulting in two separate chains with a shared history. This can occur intentionally through a planned protocol upgrade or unintentionally due to network conflicts. The significance of forking in Blockchain technology can be examined from several perspectives:

Network Upgrades and Innovation: Forking allows for the introduction of new features, improvements, and enhancements to a Blockchain network. It provides a mechanism for implementing changes to the underlying protocol, enabling developers to add functionality, improve performance, or address security vulnerabilities. Forking facilitates innovation by creating a pathway for the evolution of Blockchain technology without requiring unanimous consensus from all network participants.

Decentralization and Community Governance: Forking reinforces the decentralized nature of Blockchain systems. It empowers the community of users, miners, and developers to influence the direction of the network. In a Blockchain network, no single entity controls the direction of development. When disagreements arise, forking allows for alternative paths to be explored. In addition to ensuring that the network can adjust to the requirements and preferences of its users, this encourages community governance.

Consensus and Network Security: Forking serves as a security measure to protect the integrity of the Blockchain network. If there is a network attack or a significant disagreement among nodes, forking can be used to isolate malicious or unwanted behavior. By forking the chain, honest nodes can continue operating on the new branch, maintaining the network's security and integrity. This capability demonstrates the Blockchain's resilience against potential threats and ensures that consensus is maintained.

Community and Ecosystem Development: Forking can lead to the creation of new Blockchain communities and ecosystems. When a fork occurs, it presents an opportunity for developers, investors, and users to explore alternative paths and experiment with new ideas. This can foster innovation, attract new participants, and create diverse Blockchain platforms, each with its own unique features and value propositions.

Bug Fixes and Compatibility: Forking enables the swift implementation of critical bug fixes and compatibility updates. In the event of a discovered vulnerability or issue, a fork can be used to deploy a network-wide patch, ensuring the Blockchain's security and stability.

User and Investor Choice: Forking provides users and investors with options and flexibility. When a Blockchain forks, token holders typically retain an equal amount of the new forked coin, giving them the choice to support and engage with the new chain or stick with the original. This market dynamics and user preferences drive the direction and value of the forked chains.

Forking in Blockchain technology holds significant importance as it enables network upgrades, fosters decentralization and community governance, enhances security, and drives innovation. It is a powerful tool that shapes the evolution of Blockchain networks and contributes to their resilience and adaptability.

5.2.3 Advantages and Disadvantage of Forking

Forks, or forking, refers to a point on a Blockchain where the ledger splits into two potential paths forward, resulting in two separate chains. This can occur intentionally or unintentionally, and it can have both advantages and disadvantages.

Advantages of Forks in Blockchain Technology:

Redundancy and Security: Forks provide Blockchain networks with redundancy and security. Unintentional forks can occur due to network latency or conflicts in the ordering of transactions. Having forks ensures that if one chain becomes compromised or experiences issues, the network can continue operating without disruption by switching to the alternative chain.

Consensus and Upgrades: Intentional forks, often referred to as "hard forks," are used to implement significant upgrades or changes to a Blockchain's protocol. Hard forks allow for the introduction of new features, improvements, and bug fixes, enabling the evolution and adaptation of Blockchain technology.

Community Decision-making: Forks can empower the community of users and stakeholders in a Blockchain network. If a proposed change is controversial or not unanimously agreed upon, a fork allows for the coexistence of different versions of the Blockchain, respecting the preferences of different user groups.

Innovation and Experimentation: Forks facilitate innovation and the exploration of new ideas. They provide a mechanism for testing and experimenting with alternative protocols, consensus mechanisms, or features without affecting the entire network.

Disadvantages of Forks in Blockchain Technology:

Network Instability: Unintentional forks can lead to temporary network instability, especially if they occur frequently or persist for extended periods. These factors can lead to delays in confirming transactions and potentially increased fees.

Chain Splits and Confusion: In the case of hard forks, if all nodes or participants do not agree to adopt the new rules, a permanent split in the Blockchain can occur. This can lead to confusion among users, especially newcomers, regarding which chain to follow and can potentially result in economic losses.

Centralization Concerns: Hard forks that are not properly coordinated or communicated can lead to centralization risks. Larger mining pools or stakeholders with significant influence might favor one chain over another, potentially affecting the decentralized nature of the network.

Resource Requirements: Forks, especially hard forks, require all nodes to update their software to remain compatible with the network. This can be challenging for smaller participants or those with limited technical expertise, potentially leading to reduced participation and network fragmentation.

Reputation and Trust: Frequent or controversial forks might impact the reputation and trust in a particular Blockchain network, potentially affecting its adoption and long-term viability.

Forks in Blockchain technology have advantages in terms of security, upgrades, and community decision-making, but they also come with challenges related to network stability, chain splits, centralization risks, resource requirements, and potential trust issues. Proper governance mechanisms and careful planning are essential to mitigate the disadvantages and harness the benefits of forking.

Sales

5.3 Introduction

Sales in the context of Blockchain technology refer to the promotion, selling, and adoption of Blockchain-based solutions, services, or products to individuals, businesses, or organizations. This emerging field involves leveraging the unique attributes of Blockchain—such as decentralization, transparency, security, and efficiency—to attract and convince potential clients to integrate these technologies into their existing systems or processes. The primary objective of Blockchain sales professionals is to demonstrate the transformative potential of Blockchain technology. Blockchain solutions encompass a wide range of applications, including decentralized finance (DeFi), smart contracts, distributed ledger systems, cryptocurrency wallets, and non-fungible tokens (NFTs). Each of these solutions offers distinct advantages, from enhanced security and trust to improved transparency and traceability in transactions. Sales teams must articulate these benefits clearly to prospective customers, addressing their specific needs and challenges. A critical component of Blockchain sales is education and awareness. Given the technical complexity and novelty of Blockchain technology, sales professionals must demystify its concepts and present them in an accessible manner. This involves highlighting real-world use cases and success stories that illustrate how Blockchain can drive efficiency, reduce costs, enhance security, and enable innovative business models. Identifying and understanding the target audience is essential in Blockchain sales. The audience can range from individual investors and enthusiasts interested in cryptocurrencies and NFTs to enterprises exploring Blockchain for supply chain management or data security, and even government organizations seeking transparent and tamper-proof record-keeping systems. Each segment has unique requirements and concerns that sales teams must address. Moreover, staying abreast of regulatory and compliance issues is crucial. Blockchain technology operates in a complex and evolving legal landscape, particularly concerning cryptocurrencies and financial transactions. Sales professionals must ensure that their solutions adhere to regulatory frameworks and provide assurance of compliance to potential clients. Building trust and forming strategic partnerships are also pivotal. Given the relatively nascent stage of Blockchain technology, establishing credibility through transparent communication, reliable performance, and demonstrating the integrity of Blockchain solutions can significantly enhance sales efforts.

5.3.1 Definitions

Sales on a Blockchain platform offer a decentralized and secure environment for buyers and sellers to interact directly, fostering trust and transparency. Smart contracts self-execute agreements, streamlining the sales process and reducing intermediaries.

Vitalik Buterin

Utilizing Blockchain technology ensures that sales transactions are secure, transparent, and resistant to tampering. Each sale is documented on a decentralized ledger, guaranteeing auditability and traceability. This enhances trust and minimizes conflicts between buyers and sellers.

Christine Moy

5.3.2 Key concepts of sales in the Blockchain

Blockchain Solutions: Blockchain technology offers a range of solutions such as decentralized finance (DeFi), smart contracts, distributed ledger systems, cryptocurrency wallets, and non-fungible tokens (NFTs). Sales professionals in this field would focus on promoting and explaining the benefits of these innovative solutions to potential clients.

Target Audience: The target audience for Blockchain sales can vary widely. It may include individual investors interested in cryptocurrencies and NFTs, businesses exploring Blockchain for supply chain management or data security, or government organizations looking to implement Blockchain for record-keeping and transparent transactions.

Educating and Awareness: A significant part of sales in Blockchain technology involves educating potential customers about the complex concepts underlying this emerging field. Sales professionals need to simplify and communicate the advantages, security, and transparency that Blockchain brings to various industries.

Demonstrating Use Cases: To convince potential clients, it is essential to showcase successful use cases and real-world applications of Blockchain technology. This could include examples of improved efficiency, cost reduction, enhanced security, or innovative business models enabled by Blockchain solutions.

Regulatory and Compliance Considerations: Sales professionals need to stay updated on the evolving regulatory landscape surrounding Blockchain and cryptocurrencies. They must ensure that the solutions they offer comply with legal and regulatory frameworks, especially in the financial industry.

Building Trust and Partnerships: Given the relatively new nature of Blockchain technology, building trust with potential customers is crucial. Sales strategies may involve forming strategic partnerships, providing transparent information, and highlighting the security and integrity that Blockchain solutions offer.

Customization and Tailored Solutions: Understanding the specific needs of clients is essential. Sales professionals work closely with potential customers to tailor Blockchain solutions to their unique requirements, ensuring a good fit and maximizing the benefits they can derive from adopting Blockchain technology.

Sales in Blockchain technology require a combination of technical knowledge, strong communication skills, and the ability to build trust and partnerships in a rapidly evolving industry.

5.3.3 Types of Sales

The manner in which sales and transactions are conducted has been transformed by Blockchain technology, which provides enhanced levels of security, transparency, and decentralisation. Here are some key types of sales commonly associated with Blockchain technology:

Token Sales or Initial Coin Offerings (ICOs): Token sales, or ICOs, are unique to the Blockchain industry and are a popular method for startups and decentralized projects to raise capital. In an ICO, a company creates and offers digital tokens or coins to investors in exchange for funding. These tokens may represent a form of currency, provide access to a particular service or platform, or entitle holders to certain rights within the project's ecosystem.

Decentralized Finance (DeFi) Sales: DeFi sales refer to transactions that occur within the decentralized finance sector built on Blockchain technology. In DeFi, various financial services and products, such as lending, borrowing, trading, and insurance, are accessible directly between peers without intermediaries like banks. Users can buy and sell crypto assets, participate in liquidity pools, invest in decentralized investment protocols, and more.

Non-Fungible Token (NFT) Sales: Nonfungible tokens (NFTs) are unique digital assets that represent ownership of specific items, including music, art, collectibles, virtual real estate, or even tangible assets. NFT sales involve the transfer of ownership of these tokens, usually through Blockchain-based marketplaces or auction platforms. NFTs are often sold using smart contracts, ensuring secure and transparent transactions.

Crypto Asset Sales:Crypto asset sales involve the buying and selling of various cryptocurrencies, such as Bitcoin, Ethereum, Litecoin, or any other altcoins. These sales take place on cryptocurrency exchanges or peer-to-peer trading platforms. Crypto asset sales have fueled a new form of digital currency trading and investment, offering individuals and institutions an alternative to traditional fiat currencies.

Smart Contract-Based Sales:Smart contracts are those that automatically carry out an agreement's terms and conditions. Smart contracts, which have the potential to improve sales transactions, may be developed thanks to Blockchain technology. As an observer, one can see how a smart contract is capable of executing payment once specific conditions are met. This eliminates the necessity for middlemen and strengthens confidence in the sales procedure.

Decentralized Marketplace Sales: Blockchain technology enables the development of decentralized marketplaces where buyers and sellers can connect directly without centralized intermediaries. These marketplaces can be used for various purposes, including e-commerce, peer-to-peer services, digital asset trading, or even hiring freelancers. Sales on these platforms are often conducted using cryptocurrencies.

These are just a few types of sales enabled or enhanced by Blockchain technology. The intrinsic features of Blockchain, such as immutability, transparency, and distributed ledger technology, possess the capability to transform sales procedures across various sectors and establish transaction systems that are both more secure and efficient.

5.3.4 Advantages of Sales

Blockchain technology offers several advantages when applied to sales and business transactions. Here are some key benefits:

Enhanced Security and Trust:Blockchain provides a secure and tamper-proof way to record transactions. Each transaction is cryptographically secured and linked to the previous one, creating an immutable audit trail. This mitigates the risk of fraud, improves data integrity, and fosters trust among all parties involved in the sales process.

Transparency and Traceability:The distributed nature of Blockchain allows for transparent tracking of transactions and assets. All participants in the network can view the transaction history, improving traceability and enabling better supply chain management. This transparency can help verify the legitimacy of products, improve recall processes, and enhance consumer confidence.

Smart Contracts and Automating Sales Procedures:The use of smart contracts—contracts that may self-execute depending on pre-established criteria—is made possible by Blockchain technology. Smart contracts can automate a wide range of sales procedures, including order fulfilment, payment processing, and loyalty program rewards. By automating these tasks, businesses can reduce administrative burdens, minimize errors, and improve efficiency.

Reduced Intermediaries and Costs:Blockchain technology has the potential to diminish the need for intermediaries like third-party payment processors or escrow services. By directly connecting buyers and sellers, Blockchain reduces transaction costs, streamlines the sales process, and simplifies supply chain management. This disintermediation can also lead to faster settlement times and improved cash flow.

Improved Customer Experience:Blockchain technology can enhance the customer experience by providing faster, more secure, and transparent transactions. Customers can track their purchases, verify the authenticity of products, and benefit from reduced transaction fees. Additionally, Blockchain-based loyalty programs can offer more attractive rewards, further increasing customer satisfaction and retention.

Fraud Detection and Prevention:The immutable nature of Blockchain makes it an effective tool for fraud detection and prevention. By recording transactions on a distributed ledger, it becomes easier to identify and detect suspicious activities or double-spending attempts. This enhances the security of the sales process and protects businesses and customers from fraudulent activities.

Access to New Markets:It can facilitate transnational transactions and provide access to previously untapped markets. It enables secure and cost-effective money transfers, simplifies regulatory compliance, and opens up opportunities for the benefit of global commerce, particularly for "small and medium-sized enterprises".

5.3.4 Disadvantages of sales in Blockchain Technology

Slow Transaction Speeds:The limitation of Blockchain technology resides in its sluggish transaction pace. Verifying and securing transactions via consensus mechanisms often consumes more time compared to conventional centralized systems, particularly in Blockchains featuring larger block sizes or employing energy-intensive consensus protocols like proof-of-work. Such tardiness in transaction speeds can impede its suitability for high-frequency trading or point-of-sale transactions.

Energy Consumption and Environmental Impact: Blockchain technology, especially public Blockchains that utilize proof-of-work consensus mechanisms, has been criticized for its high energy consumption and environmental impact. The computational power required to solve complex cryptographic puzzles and validate transactions can lead to substantial electricity usage. As such, Concerns have arisen regarding the sustainable longevity and ecological consequences of Blockchain technology, especially amidst the growing acceptance of cryptocurrencies.

Regulatory and Legal Uncertainties: The decentralized nature of Blockchain technology presents regulatory and legal challenges. The lack of centralized control makes it difficult for governments and regulatory bodies to oversee and enforce laws related to money laundering, taxation, and consumer protection. This regulatory uncertainty has led to varying levels of acceptance and adoption across different jurisdictions.

Complexity and User Experience: Blockchains can be complex systems that require specialized knowledge to navigate and use effectively. The technology stack involved in Blockchain implementations can be daunting for users who are not familiar with cryptographic concepts, wallet management, private keys, and transaction processes. Improving user interfaces and simplifying the user experience is an ongoing area of focus to encourage wider adoption.

Scalability and Interoperability Concerns: While Blockchain technology offers scalability improvements over traditional databases, scaling a Blockchain network to handle a large volume of transactions while maintaining decentralization and security remains a challenge. Moreover, the seamless interoperability across various Blockchain platforms and existing legacy systems remains a challenge, impeding the smooth exchange of data and constraining the broader adoption potential.

Security and Privacy Risks: Despite the built-in security features of Blockchain technology, there remain potential risks related to vulnerabilities in smart contracts, the management of private keys, and the threat of cyber-attacks. Further, while Blockchain provides pseudonymity, the public nature of transactions on a distributed ledger can raise privacy concerns, especially when sensitive data is involved.

Cost Implications: Implementing and maintaining a Blockchain network can be costly, especially for smaller organizations or start-ups. The resources required to run nodes, develop smart contracts, and ensure network security can be significant. Additionally, the volatility of cryptocurrency prices can impact the value of transactions, potentially affecting revenue streams.

References

- Alzhrani, F., Saeedi, K., & Zhao, L. (2024). A process-aware framework to support Process Mining from Blockchain applications. *Journal of King Saud University-Computer and Information Sciences, 36*(2), 101956.
- Azad, P., Akcora, C. G., & Khan, A. (2024). Machine Learning for Blockchain Data Analysis: Progress and Opportunities. *arXiv preprint arXiv:2404.18251.*
- Chithaluru, P., Al-Turjman, F., Dugyala, R., Stephan, T., Kumar, M., & Dhatterwal, J. S. (2024). An enhanced consortium Blockchain diversity mining technique for IoT metadata aggregation. *Future Generation Computer Systems, 152*, 239-253.
- Chithaluru, P., Al-Turjman, F., Dugyala, R., Stephan, T., Kumar, M., & Dhatterwal, J. S. (2024). An enhanced consortium Blockchain diversity mining technique for IoT metadata aggregation. *Future Generation Computer Systems, 152*, 239-253.
- Chithaluru, P., Al-Turjman, F., Dugyala, R., Stephan, T., Kumar, M., & Dhatterwal, J. S. (2024). An enhanced consortium Blockchain diversity mining technique for IoT metadata aggregation. *Future Generation Computer Systems, 152*, 239-253.
- Fang, X., & Li, M. (2024). Privacy-Preserving Process Mining: A Blockchain-Based Privacy-Aware Reversible Shared Image Approach. *Applied Artificial Intelligence, 38*(1), 2321556.
- Gudimetla, S. S. V., & Tirumalaraju, N. (2024). Blockchain Technology and Data Mining Tools for Combating Fraud: With Reference to the Banking Sector. In *Frameworks for Blockchain Standards, Tools, Testbeds, and Platforms* (pp. 49-72). IGI Global.
- Hasan, K. M. B., Sajid, M., Lapina, M. A., Shahid, M., & Kotecha, K. (2024). Blockchain technology meets 6 G wireless networks: A systematic survey. *Alexandria Engineering Journal, 92*, 199-220.
- Hasan, K. M. B., Sajid, M., Lapina, M. A., Shahid, M., & Kotecha, K. (2024). Blockchain technology meets 6 G wireless networks: A systematic survey. *Alexandria Engineering Journal, 92*, 199-220.
- Kaur, M., & Gupta, S. (2024). Blockchain technology: An overview with notable features and challenges. *Artificial Intelligence, Blockchain, Computing and Security Volume 2*, 186-193.
- Onifade, M., Adebisi, J. A., & Zvarivadza, T. (2024). Recent advances in Blockchain technology: prospects, applications and constraints in the minerals industry. *International Journal of Mining, Reclamation and Environment*, 1-37.

- Onifade, M., Adebisi, J. A., & Zvarivadza, T. (2024). Recent advances in Blockchain technology: prospects, applications and constraints in the minerals industry. *International Journal of Mining, Reclamation and Environment*, 1-37.
- Porfirenko, V., Melnyk, M., Ivanov, V., Hobta, M., Diachenko, T., & Vysochylo, O. (2024). Organization and Features of Investing in the Cryptocurrency Market in Ukraine. In *Intelligent Systems, Business, and Innovation Research* (pp. 213-225). Cham: Springer Nature Switzerland.
- Ressi, D., Romanello, R., Piazza, C., & Rossi, S. (2024). AI-enhanced Blockchain technology: A review of advancements and opportunities. *Journal of Network and Computer Applications*, 103858.
- Rosales, A., Millar, H., & Richardson, A. (2024). Leveraging intra-provincial regulatory differences in a post-Paris context: Cryptocurrency mining "reverse battery" strategy in Atlantic Canada. *The Extractive Industries and Society*, *17*, 101396.
- Shakadwipi, A. J., Jain, D. C., & Nagini, S. (2024). Fraud Detection System for Identity Crime using Blockchain Technology and Data Mining Algorithms. *International Journal of Intelligent Systems and Applications in Engineering*, *12*(9s), 247-251.
- Zhao, X., Zhang, G., Long, H. W., & Si, Y. W. (2024). Minimizing block incentive volatility through Verkle tree-based dynamic transaction storage. *Decision Support Systems*, *180*, 114180.
- Abellán Álvarez, I., Gramlich, V., & Sedlmeir, J. (2024, April). Unsealing the secrets of Blockchain consensus: A systematic comparison of the formal security of proof-of-work and proof-of-stake. In *Proceedings of the 39th ACM/SIGAPP Symposium on Applied Computing* (pp. 278-287).
- Álvarez, I. A., Gramlich, V., & Sedlmeir, J. (2024). Unsealing the secrets of Blockchain consensus: A systematic comparison of the formal security of proof-of-work and proof-of-stake. *arXiv preprint arXiv:2401.14527*.
- Alzoubi, Y. I., & Mishra, A. (2024). Techniques to alleviate Blockchain bloat: Potentials, challenges, and recommendations. *Computers and Electrical Engineering*, *116*, 109216.
- Ba, C. T., Dileo, M., Galdeman, A., Zignani, M., & Gaito, S. (2024). Analyzing user migration in Blockchain online social networks through network structure and discussion topics of communities on multilayer networks. *Distributed Ledger Technologies: Research and Practice*.
- Devi, V. S., Rammohan, S. R., Sheela, K., Vaidehi, V., & Jayashri, N. (2024). ODBFT: An Optimal Derivative based Byzantine Fault Tolerance of

Blockchain Consensus Algorithm with Smart Digital Contract for Health Monitoring System. *International Journal of Intelligent Systems and Applications in Engineering, 12*(17s), 766-780.

- Dwivedi, K., Agrawal, A., Bhatia, A., & Tiwari, K. (2024). A Novel Classification of Attacks on Blockchain Layers: Vulnerabilities, Attacks, Mitigations, and Research Directions. *arXiv preprint arXiv:2404.18090.*
- Farah, M. B., Ahmed, Y., Mahmoud, H., Shah, S. A., Al-kadri, M. O., Taramonli, S., ... & Aneiba, A. (2024). A survey on Blockchain technology in the maritime industry: Challenges and future perspectives. *Future Generation Computer Systems.*
- Gadiraju, D. S., & Aggarwal, V. (2024). Prism Blockchain Enabled Internet of Things with Deep Reinforcement Learning. *Blockchain: Research and Applications,* 100205.
- Garg, S., Kumar Kaushal, R., Kumar, N., & Boonchieng, E. (2024). Exploring Research Challenges of Blockchain and Supporting Technology with Potential Solution in Healthcare. *International Journal of Computing and Digital Systems, 16*(1), 487-507.
- Gol, D. A., & Gondaliya, N. (2024). Blockchain: A comparative analysis of hybrid consensus algorithm and performance evaluation. *Computers and Electrical Engineering, 117,* 108934.
- Jones, E., & Marmsoler, D. (2024). Towards Mechanised Consensus in Isabelle. In *5th International Workshop on Formal Methods for Blockchains (FMBC 2024).* Schloss Dagstuhl–Leibniz-Zentrum für Informatik.
- Kong, X., Ma, C., Ren, Y. S., Baltas, K., & Narayan, S. (2024). A comparative analysis of the price explosiveness in Bitcoin and forked coins. *Finance Research Letters, 61,* 104955.
- Kumari, S., & Patil, M. E. (2024). Academic and Commercial Circles in Block Chain Secure Privacy and Scalability at Block Chain Technologies. *International Journal of Intelligent Systems and Applications in Engineering, 12*(13s), 440-459.
- Naz, S., & Lee, S. U. J. (2024). Sea Shield: A Blockchain Technology Consensus to Improve Proof-of-Stake-Based Consensus Blockchain Safety. *Mathematics, 12*(6), 833.
- Obaid, M. K., Abood, B. S. Z., Alazzai, W. K., & Jasim, L. (2024). From Field to Fork: The Role of AI and IoT in Agriculture. In *E3S Web of Conferences* (Vol. 491, p. 02006). EDP Sciences.
- Ovezik, C., Karakostas, D., & Kiayias, A. (2024). SoK: A stratified approach to Blockchain decentralization. In *Financial Cryptography and Data*

Security 2024: Twenty-Eighth International Conference. Springer.

- Perazzo, P., & Xefraj, R. (2024). SmartFly: Fork-Free Super-Light Ethereum Classic Clients for the Internet of Things. *IEEE Internet of Things Journal.*
- Raj, R., Singh, A., Kumar, V., & Verma, P. (2024). Challenges in adopting Blockchain technology in supply chain management: a too far fetched idea?. *International Journal of Quality & Reliability Management.*
- Sharma, V., Agarwal, A., & Barua, A. (2024). Demand-Side Effects of Open Innovation: The Case of Cryptocurrency Forking. *Forthcoming, Management Science.*
- Takale, D. G., Mahalle, P. N., & Sule, B. Blockchain-Powered Direct Farm-to-Consumer Supply Chains.
- van Vulpen, P., Siu, J., & Jansen, S. (2024). Governance of decentralized autonomous organizations that produce open source software. *Blockchain: Research and Applications,* 5(1), 100166.
- Vishwakarma, L., Das, D., Das, S. K., & Becker, C. (2024, January). SmartGrid-NG: Blockchain Protocol for Secure Transaction Processing in Next Generation Smart Grid. In *Proceedings of the 25th International Conference on Distributed Computing and Networking* (pp. 174-185).
- Wang, K., Feng, G., Ji, Z., Tu, Z., & He, S. (2024). SP-PoR: Improve Blockchain performance by semi-parallel processing transactions. *Computer Networks, 245,* 110394.
- Wardhana, C. S. (2024). Eksplorasi Fundamental Cryptocurrency dalam Volatilitas Harga. *Jurnal Syntax Admiration,* 5(4), 1040-1053.
- Werbach, K., De Filippi, P., Tan, J., & Pieters, G. (2024). Blockchain Governance in the Wild.
- Wu, X., Deng, W., Quan, Y., & Zhang, L. (2024). Trust Dynamics and Market Behavior in Cryptocurrency: A Comparative Study of Centralized and Decentralized Exchanges. *arXiv preprint arXiv:2404.17227.*
- Zhu, G., He, D., An, H., Luo, M., & Peng, C. (2024). The governance technology for Blockchain systems: a survey. *Frontiers of Computer Science, 18*(2), 182813.
- Adelekan, O. A., Adisa, O., Ilugbusi, B. S., Obi, O. C., Awonuga, K. F., Asuzu, O. F., & Ndubuisi, N. L. (2024). EVOLVING TAX COMPLIANCE IN THE DIGITAL ERA: A COMPARATIVE ANALYSIS OF AI-DRIVEN MODELS AND BLOCKCHAIN TECHNOLOGY IN US TAX ADMINISTRATION. *Computer Science & IT Research Journal,* 5(2), 311-335.
- Alexander, C., & Dakos, M. (2024). The new tokenomics of crowdfunding. *British Journal of Management, 35*(2), 644-662.

- Almahadeen, L. (2024). Digital Investigation Forensic Model with P2P Timestamp Blockchain for Monitoring and Analysis. *J. Electrical Systems, 20*(1), 09-17.
- Ani, N., Millah, S., & Sunarya, P. A. (2024). Optimizing Online Business Security with Blockchain Technology. *Startupreneur Business Digital (SABDA Journal), 3*(1), 67-80.
- Beveridge, I., Angelis, J., & Mihajlov, M. (2024). Benefits and challenges with Blockchain technology in global food supply chains: views from the practice. *British Food Journal.*
- Bhuiyan, M. R. I., & Akter, M. S. (2024). Assessing the Potential Usages of Blockchain to Transform Smart Bangladesh: A PRISMA Based Systematic Review. *Journal of Information Systems and Informatics, 6*(1), 245-269.
- Drummen, M. C. H. (2024). Quantitative Analysis of the Financial Impact of Non-Fungible Token Integration on Publicly Traded Brands.
- El Madhoun, N., & Hammi, B. (2024, January). Blockchain technology in the healthcare sector: overview and security analysis. In *2024 IEEE 14th annual computing and communication workshop and conference (CCWC)* (pp. 0439-0446). IEEE.
- Elsden, C., Morgan, E., Tallyn, E., Black, S. R., Disley, M., Schafer, B., ... & Speed, C. (2024). A Token Gesture: Non-Transferable NFTs, Digital Possessions and Ownership Design. *Proceedings of the ACM on Human-Computer Interaction, 8*(CSCW1), 1-29.
- Etro, L. L., Sacco, P. L., Sironi, E., Taccalite, N., & Teti, E. (2024). Exuberance by design? Hyping cryptocurrencies markets through token underpricing. *Economics of Innovation and New Technology, 33*(3), 401-416.
- Fairuz, W. (2024). From Trust to Transformation: The Influence of Technology on Global Business Relations.
- Fang, X. (2024). Blockchain applications and supply chain performance: evidence from Chinese firms. *Technology Analysis & Strategic Management*, 1-16.
- Fohrer, N., Gade, A., & Muschkiet, M. (2024). Digitalization in logistics for textiles–possible fields of application for the Blockchain technology. *Communications in Development and Assembling of Textile Products, 5*(1), 38-47.
- Gartner, J., & Moro, A. (2024). C-level managers and born-digitals' scaling: The case of Initial Coin Offerings (ICOs). *Technological Forecasting and Social Change, 198*, 122943.

- Govindan, K., Jain, P., Singh, R. K., & Mishra, R. (2024). Blockchain technology as a strategic weapon to bring procurement 4.0 truly alive: Literature review and future research agenda. *Transportation Research Part E: Logistics and Transportation Review, 181*, 103352.
- Harvey, C. R., & Rabetti, D. (2024). International business and decentralized finance. *Journal of International Business Studies*, 1-24.
- Jang, H. W., Yoo, J. J. E., & Cho, M. (2024). Resistance to Blockchain adoption in the foodservice industry: moderating roles of public pressures and climate change awareness. *International Journal of Contemporary Hospitality Management, 36*(5), 1467-1489.
- Jiang, L., & Zhou, B. (2024). Research on pricing strategy of dual-channel supply chain based on Blockchain technology under carbon trading. *International Journal of Global Economics and Management, 2*(3), 270-279.
- Kaukonen, J. (2024). Marketing in Web 3.0: Leveraging Non-Fungible Tokens (NFTs).
- Kim, H., Hong, S. P., & Majer, M. (2024). Smart Contract Mechanism in Semiconductor Procurement System. *Nanotechnology Perceptions*, 128-141.
- Kotiloglu, S., & Ometto, M. P. (2024). An exploratory look at the role of ownership in initial coin offerings (ICO): Different audiences and ICO success. *Journal of Business Venturing Insights, 21*, e00438.
- Kräussl, R., & Tugnetti, A. (2024). Non-fungible tokens (NFTs): A review of pricing determinants, applications and opportunities. *Journal of Economic Surveys, 38*(2), 555-574.
- Kumar, A., & Anitha, J. (2024). Decentralized Application for Selling Agricultural Production through Block Chain. *International Journal of Intelligent Systems and Applications in Engineering, 12*(7s), 472-479.
- Liu, N., & Tsai, W. T. (2024). SmartDED: A Blockchain-and Smart Contract-Based Digital Electronic Detonator Safety Supervision System. *Future Internet, 16*(5), 171.
- Ma, D., Ma, P., & Hu, J. (2024). The Impact of Blockchain Technology Adoption on an E-Commerce Closed-Loop Supply Chain Considering Consumer Trust. *Sustainability, 16*(4), 1535.
- Manteghi, Y., Arkat, J., & Mahmoodi, A. (2024). Organic production competitiveness: A bi-level model integrating government policy, sustainability objectives, and Blockchain transparency. *Computers & Industrial Engineering, 191*, 110147.
- Markad, H. D., & Sakhare, S. R. (2024). IoT Supply Chain Management using Customized Blockchain Implementation. *International Journal of*

Intelligent Systems and Applications in Engineering, *12*(10s), 539-550.

- MEDINA, M. J., Baudet, C., & Lebraty, J. F. (2024). Blockchain and agency theory in supply chain management: A question of trust. *International Journal of Information Management*, 102747.
- Mohammed, N. S., Dawood, O. A., Sagheer, A. M., & Nafea, A. A. (2024). Secure Smart Contract Based on Blockchain to Prevent the Non-Repudiation Phenomenon. *Baghdad Science Journal*, *21*(1), 0234-0234.
- Obinna, F. N., Kaegon, L. E. S., & Nwafor, S. O. (2024). Innovating Intellectual Property Commercialization Models through Blockchain Technology in Public Universities in Rivers State.
- Onifade, M., Adebisi, J. A., & Zvarivadza, T. (2024). Recent advances in Blockchain technology: prospects, applications and constraints in the minerals industry. *International Journal of Mining, Reclamation and Environment*, 1-37.
- Ouriat, A., Mirarab Baygi, S. A., & Khandan Alamdari, S. (2024). Application, Pros and Cons of Blockchain Networks. *International Journal of Finance & Managerial Accounting*, *9*(35), 189-206.
- Parhamfar, M., Sadeghkhani, I., & Adeli, A. M. (2024). Towards the net zero carbon future: A review of Blockchain-enabled peer-to-peer carbon trading. *Energy Science & Engineering*.
- Parrondo, L. (2024). Typology and classification of crypto-assets based on the MiCA regulatory framework: contributions and limitations. In *Research Handbook on Financial Accounting* (pp. 264-282). Edward Elgar Publishing.
- Rathore, S., & Gupta, A. Decentralized Finance (DeFi): The Future of Finance. *ANNUAL RESEARCH JOURNAL OF SCMS, PUNE*, 171.
- Ravichandra, T., Madaan, V., Sharma, A., Deshmukh, S., Agrawal, R., Gumber, G., & Khan, M. A. (2024). A Study on Individual Awareness and Perception Towards Blockchain Technology in India. *International Journal of Intelligent Systems and Applications in Engineering*, *12*(8s), 239-250.
- Ray, R. K., Chowdhury, F. R., & Hasan, M. R. (2024). Blockchain Applications in Retail Cybersecurity: Enhancing Supply Chain Integrity, Secure Transactions, and Data Protection. *Journal of Business and Management Studies*, *6*(1), 206-214.
- Rijanto, A. (2024). Blockchain technology roles to overcome accounting, accountability and assurance barriers in supply chain finance. *Asian Review of Accounting*.

- Shahzad, K., Helo, P., Ranta, M., & Nousiainen, E. (2024). Blockchain technology for operational excellence and supply chain resilience: a framework based on use cases and an architecture demonstration. *Technology Analysis & Strategic Management*, 1-18.
- Shahzad, K., Khan, S. A., & Iqbal, A. (2024). Effects of Blockchain technology (BT) on the university librarians and libraries: a systematic literature review (SLR). *Library Hi Tech.*
- Shaik, J., & Athithan, S. (2024). Utilizing Blockchain Technology and Machine Learning for Quality Evaluation in Agricultural Supply Chains. *International Journal of Computing and Digital Systems, 16*(1), 1-14.
- Toorajipour, R., Oghazi, P., & Palmié, M. (2024). Data ecosystem business models: Value propositions and value capture with Artificial Intelligence of Things. *International Journal of Information Management, 78*, 102804.
- Vazquez Melendez, E. I., Bergey, P., & Smith, B. (2024). Blockchain technology for supply chain provenance: increasing supply chain efficiency and consumer trust. *Supply Chain Management: An International Journal.*
- Venema, P., & Wijngaarden, Y. (2024). Blockchain to blockchange? NFTs and DIY entrepreneurship in music production. *DIY, Alternative Cultures & Society*, 27538702241252874.
- Wang, S., Zhou, M., & Xiang, S. (2024). Blockchain-Enabled Utility Optimization for Supply Chain Finance: An Evolutionary Game and Smart Contract Based Approach. *Mathematics, 12*(8), 1243.
- Wasilewski, A., & Kolaczek, G. (2024). One Size Does Not Fit All: Multivariant User Interface Personalization in E-commerce. *IEEE Access.*
- Wiwoho, J., Trinugroho, I., Kharisma, D. B., & Suwadi, P. (2024). Islamic crypto assets and regulatory framework: evidence from Indonesia and global approaches. *International Journal of Law and Management, 66*(2), 155-171.
- Zhao, Q., Fan, Z. P., & Sun, M. (2024). Sales mode selection and Blockchain technology adoption decisions in a platform supply chain. *International Journal of Production Economics, 272*, 109255.

Digital Signatures

LEARNING OBJECTIVES

- Explain the role of digital signatures in ensuring the authenticity and integrity of transactions on the blockchain.
- Describe the process of creating and verifying digital signatures in blockchain transactions
- Analyze the benefits of using digital signatures over traditional signatures in blockchain transactions.
- How do digital signatures prevent tampering and fraud in blockchain transactions?

6.0 Introduction

In the rapidly evolving landscape of digital transactions, the integration of digital signatures stands as a cornerstone, ensuring the veracity, security, and efficiency of modern commerce. In this technological evolution lies Blockchain, a distributed ledger system revolutionizing how we exchange value and authenticate transactions. Digital signatures, fortified by public-key cryptography, serve as the guardians of integrity in this decentralized realm, providing incontrovertible proof of origin and authenticity. Digital signatures, akin to unique cryptographic fingerprints, encode the identity and intent of the sender, safeguarding against tampering and fraud. They operate through a sophisticated process of key generation, encryption, and verification, establishing trust in a trustless environment. Each transaction, whether a financial exchange or a smart contract execution, bears the indelible mark of its originator, ensuring accountability and transparency.

Digital Signature Explanation:

A digital signature is akin to a digital "fingerprint" or a secure, encrypted signature attached to a digital message or transaction. It is created using cryptographic algorithms that transform the sender's information, such as their private key, into a unique signature. This signature verifies the sender's identity, ensuring that the transaction or message originated from them and has not been altered during transmission.

6.1 Definitions

Digital signatures in Blockchain technology are "electronic signatures that utilize public-key cryptography to securely sign and verify transactions, ensuring the authenticity and integrity of the transmitted data.

Wang and Liu

Cryptographic signatures that are uniquely generated for each transaction, ensuring the identity and intent of the signer, and providing irrefutable proof of origin and integrity.

Lee and Kim

6.2 Key Components:

Key Pair Generation: In Blockchain, each user has a pair of cryptographic keys: a public key and a private key. These keys are mathematically linked and generated together.

Private Key Signature: When a user desires to authenticate a transaction, they employ their private key to create a unique digital signature. The private key remains secure and known only to the owner.

Public Key Verification: The recipient of the transaction utilizes the sender's public key to verify the authenticity of the digital signature. This validation process confirms that the signature corresponds to the content and remains unaltered.

Hash Function: Blockchain digital signatures often employ hash functions to enhance security. A hash function receives an input, such as transaction data, and produces a distinct hash code or fingerprint of a given length. This hash code is then signed with the private key.

Signature Verification: To verify the signature, the recipient computes the hash of the transaction data using the same hash function. They then use the sender's public key to decrypt the signature and compare the resulting hash codes. If they match, the signature is valid.

6.3 Types of Digital Signature

Blockchain technology relies heavily on a digital signature to guarantee the integrity, security, and validity of digital transactions and smart contracts. Some common types of digital signatures used in the context of

Blockchain:

Elliptic Curve Digital Signature Algorithm (ECDSA): ECDSA is widely used in Blockchain technologies, including cryptocurrencies like Bitcoin. It relies on the mathematics of elliptic curves, offering a more compact signature size compared to other algorithms. ECDSA provides enhanced safety and effectiveness, making it suitable for the verification and signing of transactions on distributed ledger systems.

RSA Digital Signature: RSA is one of the most prevalent digital signature schemes, utilizing "public-key cryptography". The system utilises a set of keys consisting of a public key for encryption and a private key for decryption and signature. RSA digital signatures are secure and flexible, accommodating various key sizes to balance security and performance. This type of digital signature is often used in Blockchain smart contracts and secure data transmission.

Digital Signature Algorithm (DSA): DSA is a digital signature standard developed by the National Institute of Standards and Technology (NIST). It utilizes discrete logarithms and finite fields, offering a secure and efficient signature scheme. DSA is commonly used in government applications and digital signature frameworks, providing authentication and integrity verification.

EdDSA (Edwards-curve Digital Signature Algorithm): EdDSA is an efficient and modern digital signature algorithm based on elliptic curve cryptography. It offers faster signing and verification speeds while providing strong security guarantees. EdDSA is designed to minimize computational requirements, making it suitable for resource-constrained devices and Blockchain applications.

Schnorr Signatures: These are considered an advanced type of digital signature scheme, offering improved efficiency and security compared to ECDSA. They provide signature aggregation, allowing multiple signatures to be combined into one, reducing data size. Schnorr signatures are gaining popularity in Blockchain technologies due to their potential for enhancing transaction speed and privacy.

Ring Signatures: Ring signatures are unique in that they provide anonymity for the signer. Instead of using a single key pair, ring signatures utilize a group of authorized public keys, any of which can be used to verify the signature. This type of signature is employed in Blockchain applications requiring privacy and confidentiality, such as certain cryptocurrency transactions.

These digital signature schemes provide the foundational security and authenticity mechanisms for Blockchain technologies, ensuring that transactions and smart contracts are tamper-proof and verifiable. Each type offers distinct advantages and use cases, contributing to the overall robustness and reliability of Blockchain systems.

6.4 How digital signatures work in the context of blockchain technology?

A digital signature is a cryptographic technique used to validate the authenticity and integrity of a message, document, or transaction. In the context of blockchain technology, digital signatures play a crucial role in ensuring the security and trustworthiness of transactions recorded on the blockchain.

Here's how digital signatures work in the context of blockchain technology:

1.**Generation**:

- When a user initiates a transaction on the blockchain, such as transferring cryptocurrency or updating a smart contract, they use their private key to generate a digital signature for the transaction.
- The private key is a unique cryptographic key known only to the user and is used to create the digital signature. It is essentially the user's digital identity and is kept secret to prevent unauthorized access.

2.**Signing the Transaction**:

- The user's private key is used in conjunction with a cryptographic algorithm (such as ECDSA - Elliptic Curve Digital Signature Algorithm) to create a unique digital signature for the transaction data.
- This digital signature is a fixed-size string of bytes that serves as a mathematical representation of the transaction and the user's authorization to perform it.

3.**Verification**:

- Once the transaction is broadcast to the blockchain network, nodes in the network verify the authenticity of the digital signature using the user's public key.

- The public key is derived from the user's private key and is freely available on the blockchain. It is used by other network participants to verify digital signatures but cannot be used to reverse-engineer the private key.
- By using the public key and the same cryptographic algorithm used to create the digital signature, nodes can confirm that the signature was indeed generated by the corresponding private key and that the transaction has not been tampered with.

4.**Validation**:

- If the digital signature is successfully verified by the network nodes, the transaction is considered valid and is added to a new block on the blockchain.
- The digital signature serves as proof of the transaction's authenticity and the user's authorization, ensuring that only the owner of the private key can initiate transactions on their behalf.
- Additionally, the digital signature ensures the integrity of the transaction data, as any modification to the transaction would result in a different digital signature, which would fail the verification process.

6.5 Use of Digital Signatures

Digital signatures are integral to many trending applications within the context of blockchain technology. Here are some examples:

1.**Decentralized Finance (DeFi)**:

- **Use**: In DeFi platforms built on blockchain, digital signatures are used to sign transactions and interact with smart contracts.
- **Example**: Users can engage in activities such as lending, borrowing, and trading cryptocurrencies on decentralized exchanges (DEXs) like Uniswap and Compound. Digital signatures authenticate these transactions, ensuring that only authorized users can execute them.

2.**Non-Fungible Tokens (NFTs)**:

- **Use**: NFT platforms rely on digital signatures to prove ownership and authenticate transactions for unique digital assets.

- **Example**: Artists can tokenize their artwork as NFTs on platforms like OpenSea and Rarible. Each NFT is associated with a digital signature that verifies the authenticity and ownership of the asset. When buying or selling NFTs, users sign transactions with their private keys to transfer ownership securely.

3.**Supply Chain Traceability**:

- **Use**: Blockchain-based supply chain platforms use digital signatures to sign and authenticate transactions related to product tracking and traceability.
- **Example**: Companies like IBM's Food Trust and VeChain use blockchain technology to track the journey of products from manufacturer to consumer. Digital signatures ensure the integrity of data recorded on the blockchain, preventing tampering and fraud throughout the supply chain.

4.**Digital Identity and Self-Sovereign Identity (SSI)**:

- **Use**: Blockchain-based identity solutions utilize digital signatures to verify and authenticate users' identities without relying on centralized authorities.
- **Example**: Projects like uPort and Sovrin enable users to create self-sovereign digital identities stored on a blockchain. Users sign authentication requests with their private keys, providing cryptographic proof of identity without sharing sensitive personal information.

5.**Smart Contracts**:

- **Use**: Smart contracts, self-executing contracts with predefined rules encoded on the blockchain, rely on digital signatures to validate and execute transactions automatically.
- **Example**: Decentralized applications (DApps) like Aave and Compound use smart contracts to automate lending and borrowing activities. Users interact with these contracts by signing transactions with their digital wallets, enabling trustless and permissionless financial services.

6.Tokenization of Assets:

- **Use**: Blockchain facilitates the tokenization of real-world assets such as real estate, stocks, and commodities, with digital signatures ensuring the authenticity and ownership of these tokenized assets.
- **Example**: Platforms like Harbor and Polymath enable the issuance and trading of tokenized securities on the blockchain. Digital signatures authenticate transactions involving these tokens, providing a secure and transparent way to transfer ownership of assets.

6.6 Advantages and Disadvantages of Digital Signature

Advantages and Disadvantages of Digital Signatures in Blockchain technology

The integration of digital signatures into Blockchain technology offers a multitude of advantages, enhancing security, efficiency, and traceability in various applications. some key benefits:

Enhanced Security: Digital signatures provide an advanced level of security for Blockchain transactions. They offer a cryptographic signature unique to each transaction, ensuring data integrity and authentication. This makes it virtually impossible for unauthorized alterations or fraud, as any alteration in the data will effect in a mismatch of the digital signature.

Decentralization and Trust: Blockchains are decentralized systems, and digital signatures further reinforce this trustless environment. Each participant can have a unique digital signature, removing the need for centralized authorities to verify identities or transactions. This distributed consensus mechanism ensures transparency and trust among users.

Automation and Efficiency: The use of digital signatures automates various processes, increasing efficiency. Smart contracts, for example, can be programmed to execute specific actions upon verification of a valid digital signature. This streamlines transactions, reduces chapterwork, and eliminates manual errors, it is perfect for electronic identification examination, supply chains management, and other applications.

Traceability and Auditability: Digital signatures provide an audit trail, allowing for the traceability of transactions. Each signature is time-stamped and linked to the previous one, creating an immutable record. This feature is valuable for regulatory compliance, dispute resolution, and ensuring accountability in industries like finance, healthcare, and government.

Cost Reduction: Through the elimination of physical signatures, travel, and manual verification processes, the use of digital signatures on a Blockchain can greatly cut expenses for both individuals and organisations.

This is particularly advantageous for international transactions, as conventional approaches may be both time-consuming and costly.

Interoperability and Integration: Digital signatures can facilitate interoperability between different Blockchain platforms and existing digital infrastructure. This enables a seamless exchange of data and transactions, improving overall efficiency and widening the scope of Blockchain technology adoption.

Digital signatures in Blockchain technology offer numerous benefits, enhancing the security, efficiency, and openness of the digital ecosystem, revolutionizing how we conduct business and exchange value.

Disadvantages of Digital Signatures in Blockchain Technology:

Regulatory and Legal Challenges: The use of digital signatures may face regulatory and legal hurdles, as not all jurisdictions have fully recognized their legality. This can create complexities, especially in cross-border transactions, where varying regional regulations and compliance standards come into play.

Infrastructure Requirements: Implementing digital signatures on a Blockchain network requires a robust infrastructure. The process involves public key infrastructure (PKI) and the management of private and public keys, which demands technical expertise and secure storage solutions to prevent key theft or loss.

Key Management and Revocation: The security and management of private keys are critical. The loss or theft of a private key has the potential to jeopardise the integrity of the entire digital signature system. Moreover, the procedure of revoking and substituting keys can be intricate and time-consuming, potentially causing interruptions to ongoing processes.

Compatibility and Standardization: Ensuring compatibility and standardization across different systems and platforms can be challenging. Inconsistent implementation of digital signature protocols may lead to interoperability issues, limiting the seamless integration and adoption of Blockchain technology.

While digital signatures in Blockchain technology offer numerous advantages, it is indispensable to prudently consider the potential drawbacks and implement robust key management systems and regulatory frameworks to mitigate risks and ensure widespread adoption.

6.7 Role of Digital signatures in preventing tampering and fraud in blockchain transactions

Digital signatures play a crucial role in preventing tampering and fraud in blockchain transactions by providing mechanisms for authentication, integrity, and non-repudiation. Here's how digital signatures achieve this:

1.**Authentication**:

- Digital signatures verify the identity of the sender and ensure that only authorized parties can initiate transactions on the blockchain.
- Each participant in the blockchain network has a unique private key that is used to generate digital signatures for transactions.
- By signing transactions with their private keys, participants cryptographically prove their identity, preventing unauthorized parties from impersonating them.

2.**Integrity**:

- Digital signatures ensure the integrity of transaction data by detecting any unauthorized changes or modifications to the transaction.
- When a transaction is signed with a digital signature, the signature is calculated based on the transaction data itself.
- Any alteration to the transaction data, such as changing the amount or recipient of a transfer, would result in a completely different digital signature.
- Nodes in the blockchain network verify the digital signature against the original transaction data to confirm that the transaction has not been tampered with.

3.**Non-repudiation**:

- Digital signatures provide non-repudiation, meaning that the sender cannot deny having signed the transaction once it has been verified by the network.
- Since digital signatures are uniquely linked to the signer's private key, they serve as cryptographic proof of the sender's authorization and involvement in the transaction.
- This prevents the sender from later claiming that they did not authorize the transaction, as the digital signature provides irrefutable evidence of their consent.

4.**Secure Verification**:

- Digital signatures rely on cryptographic algorithms that are computationally secure, making it virtually impossible for unauthorized parties to forge valid signatures without access to the signer's private key.
- The use of public key cryptography ensures that anyone can verify the authenticity of a digital signature using the corresponding public key, without needing access to the signer's private key.

References

- Banerjee, K., & Saha, S. (2024). Blockchain Signatures to Ensure Information Integrity and Non-Repudiation in the Digital Era: A comprehensive study. *International Journal of Computing and Digital Systems*, *16*(1), 1-12.
- Banerjee, K., & Saha, S. (2024). Blockchain Signatures to Ensure Information Integrity and Non-Repudiation in the Digital Era: A comprehensive study. *International Journal of Computing and Digital Systems*, *16*(1), 1-12.
- BRĂCĂCESCU, R. V., MOCANU, Ş., IONIŢĂ, A. D., & BRĂCĂCESCU, C. (2024). A PROPOSAL OF DIGITAL IDENTITY MANAGEMENT USING BLOCKCHAIN. *REVUE ROUMAINE DES SCIENCES TECHNIQUES—SÉRIE ÉLECTROTECHNIQUE ET ÉNERGÉTIQUE*, *69*(1), 85-90.
- Brunetto, C. (2024). *Distributed Verifier-Smart Contract for verifying ECDSA signatures on multiple curves* (Doctoral dissertation, Politecnico di Torino).
- Chen, J., Wang, Z., Srivastava, G., Alghamdi, T. A., Khan, F., Kumari, S., & Xiong, H. (2024). Industrial Blockchain threshold signatures in federated learning for unified space-air-ground-sea model training. *Journal of Industrial Information Integration*, *39*, 100593.
- Feng, M., Lin, C., Wu, W., & He, D. (2024). SM2-DualRing: Efficient SM2-based ring signature schemes with logarithmic size. *Computer Standards & Interfaces*, *87*, 103763.
- Grierson, S., Kasimatis, D., Buchanan, W. J., Eckl, C., Papadopoulos, P., Pitropakis, N., ... & Ghaleb, B. (2024). Anonymised Fixed-Ring Identification Using Decentralised Identifiers. *arXiv preprint arXiv:2403.05271*.

- Hasan, K. M. B., Sajid, M., Lapina, M. A., Shahid, M., & Kotecha, K. (2024). Blockchain technology meets 6 G wireless networks: A systematic survey. *Alexandria Engineering Journal, 92,* 199-220.
- Huang, Y. (2024). Smart home system using Blockchain technology in green lighting environment in rural areas. *Heliyon.*
- Javaid, M. A. R., Ashraf, M., Rehman, T., & Tariq, N. (2024). Impact of Post Quantum Digital Signatures On Block Chain: Comparative Analysis. *The Asian Bulletin of Big Data Management, 4*(1), Science-4.
- Jayakumari, B., Sheeba, S. L., Eapen, M., Anbarasi, J., Ravi, V., Suganya, A., & Jawahar, M. (2024). E-voting System using Cloud-based Hybrid Blockchain Technology. *Journal of Safety Science and Resilience.*
- Jiang, J., Gao, Y., & Li, Y. (2024). Enhancing Copyright Protection Through Blockchain and Ring Signature Algorithm From Lattice. *IEEE Access, 12,* 41247-41254.
- Kim, J., Kim, P., Lee, Y., & Choi, D. (2024). Key Backup and Recovery for Resilient DID Environment. *Mathematics, 12*(6), 830.
- Mbaidin, H., Sbaee, N., AlMubydeen, I., & Alomari, K. (2024). Key success drivers for implementation Blockchain technology in UAE Islamic banking. *Uncertain Supply Chain Management, 12*(2), 1175-1188.
- Mohammed, N. S., Dawood, O. A., Sagheer, A. M., & Nafea, A. A. (2024). Secure Smart Contract Based on Blockchain to Prevent the Non-Repudiation Phenomenon. *Baghdad Science Journal, 21*(1), 0234-0234.

- Mohammed, N. S., Dawood, O. A., Sagheer, A. M., & Nafea, A. A. (2024). Secure Smart Contract Based on Blockchain to Prevent the Non-Repudiation Phenomenon. *Baghdad Science Journal, 21*(1), 0234-0234.

- Rath, S. S., & MP, P. J. (2024). Enhancing data security in SAP-enabled healthcare systems with cryptography and digital signatures using Blockchain technology. *International Journal of Systematic Innovation, 8*(1), 36-47.

- Rath, S. S., & MP, P. J. (2024). Enhancing data security in SAP-enabled healthcare systems with cryptography and digital signatures using Blockchain technology. *International Journal of Systematic Innovation, 8*(1), 36-47.

- Song, Z. (2024, February). Educational Resource Sharing based on Blockchain Technology using Elliptical Curve Digital Signature Algorithm-Proof-of-Stake. In *2024 International Conference on Integrated Circuits and Communication Systems (ICICACS)* (pp. 1-4). IEEE.

- Tasdelen, A. (2024). Fundamentals of Blockchain. In *Exploring Blockchain Applications* (pp. 6-25). CRC Press.
- Thomas, S. (2024). FRAUD DETECTION FRAMEWORK USING PRIVACY PRESERVING RECORD LINKAGE IN TELECOM.
- Tian, H., & Wang, J. (2024). An Energy Trading Method Based on Alliance Blockchain and Multi-Signature. *Computers, Materials & Continua, 78*(2).
- Uikey, D., Brarskar, R., & Ahirwar, M. A Blockchain-Based Digital Notary System Provides Reliable and Tamper-Proof Timestamping and Verification Services for Digital Documents: A Review.
- Verma, G., & Kanrar, S. (2024). Secure document sharing model based on Blockchain technology and attribute-based encryption. *Multimedia Tools and Applications, 83*(6), 16377-16394.
- Xu, M., Guo, Y., Liu, C., Hu, Q., Yu, D., Xiong, Z., ... & Cheng, X. (2024). Exploring Blockchain technology through a modular lens: A survey. *ACM Computing Surveys, 56*(9), 1-39.
- Yuliana, M., & Walidaniy, W. D. (2024). Efficient Multi-signature and QR Code Integration for Document Authentication Using EdDSA-based Algorithm. *International Journal of Intelligent Engineering & Systems, 17*(2).
- Zhu, X., Qi, Z., Chiong, R., Zhang, P., & Ren, M. (2024). The dilemma of introducing Blockchain technology into an assembly supply chain: A double-edged sword of profit and upstream invasion. *Computers & Industrial Engineering, 188*, 109830.